Writing with style

Writing with style

Conversations on the art of writing

JOHN R. TRIMBLE

The University of Texas at Austin

PRENTICE-HALL, INC., Englewood Cliffs, New Jersey

Library of Congress Cataloging in Publication Data

TRIMBLE, JOHN R   1940–
   Writing with style.

   1. English language—Rhetoric.   2. Exposition
(Rhetoric)   3. English language—Punctuation.
I. Title.
PE1408.T69   808'.042   74–24674
ISBN   0–13–970376–4
ISBN   0–13–970368–3 pbk.

C–0–13–970376–4
P–0–13–970368–3

Library of Congress Catalog Card No.: 74–24674

Printed in the United States of America

19   18

The quotations on pages 5 and 6 are from *Deeper Into Movies* by Pauline
Kael, by permission of Little, Brown and Co. in association
with The Atlantic Monthly Press.

The quotation on page 70 is from F. Scott Fitzgerald, THE CRACK-UP.
Copyright 1945 by New Directions Publishing Corporation.
Reprinted by permission of New Directions Publishing Corporation,
and The Bodley Head Ltd.

The quotation on page 95 is from WRITERS AT WORK: The Paris
Review Interviews, Second Series. Copyright © 1963 by The Paris
Review, Inc. All rights reserved. Reprinted by permission of
The Viking Press, Inc. and Martin Secker & Warburg Limited.

The quotation from Ezra Pound's ABC OF READING, on page 131.
Copyright 1934 by Ezra Pound. Reprinted by permission of
New Directions Publishing Corporation and Faber and Faber Ltd.

Prentice-Hall International, Inc., *London*
Prentice-Hall of Australia, Pty. Ltd., *Sydney*
Prentice-Hall of Canada, Ltd., *Toronto*
Prentice-Hall of India Private Limited, *New Delhi*
Prentice-Hall of Japan, Inc., *Tokyo*

For Judy, with gratitude

Contents

A word about these "conversations"

About a year ago a bright sophomore came by my office for his first writing conference of the term. First conferences are usually slow going, and this one proved no exception. After 20 minutes we were still discussing the problems of his opening paragraph. Suddenly, his growing sense of himself as a bungler broke through his composure. He leaned back, shook his head, and said with a wan, courageous smile, "I think what I could use is a good survival kit."

That remark stayed with me, for it seemed to sum up the anguish of countless other undergraduates equally bewildered by the basics of expository writing. Perhaps you're among them. Their plight is ironic, but even more it is poignant. Theoretically, they are well trained in writing: they have years of classrooms, half a dozen textbooks, and scores of essays behind them. In reality, though, a writing assignment makes them feel as ignorant and panicky as the first day they walked into their high-school trigonometry class.

Why are they so bewildered? For some, perhaps because their textbooks haven't explained the basics to them in language they could readily understand, or even care to understand. Others, perhaps, are victims of overlong textbooks, self-defeating in their glorious comprehensiveness. (Who, after all, can distinguish the fundamental from the trivial after trudging through 500 pages of technical lore, however well presented?) The befuddlement of still others may stem from having been given the tools but never a graphic sense of how good writers actually use them. And yet another not-so-remote possibility: many of them may have been conditioned to believe that writing acceptably involves translating every thought into a dead classical tongue known as Formal English. Whatever the reason or reasons, one thing is certainly clear enough: they feel lost.

My hope is that this book—an informal, compact, practical little book styled after my own writing conferences—answers the wish for a "survival kit." I've stocked it with emergency provisions especially useful to those of you lost in the jungles of essay-writing. Many of the provisions, though, are equally useful in other desperate situations, as you will see. Above all, I've tried to equip you with advice on how to become a literary Robinson Crusoe—that is, self-sufficient. A writer isn't self-sufficient until he has learned to think well. This involves, among other things, understanding the psychological element of the whole business. As I see it, writing is applied psychology because it is the art of creating desired effects. It follows from this that our chief need is to know *what* effects are desirable and *how* to create them. Thus this book: a blend of commonsense theory and practical suggestions.

Specifically, I tried to do four things here:

1 Explain how experienced writers think.
2 Share a number of useful tips on writing.
3 Answer some of the most recurring questions about punctuation, conventions, and stylistic taboos.
4 Keep it all brief enough to be read over a couple of cups of coffee.

Now that the book is finished, I see that you'll probably need a third, maybe even a fourth cup to see you through. For that I apologize. The book became a friend I was loath to bid good-bye to.

I suppose a few readers—teachers mainly—may be disappointed that I've excluded end-of-chapter exercises, not to mention discussion of research papers, grammar, syllogistic reasoning, patterns of "paragraph movement," and other such things conventionally covered by textbooks on writing. I can only answer that this is not—and doesn't want to be—a conventional textbook on writing. There are plenty of those already, and no need to duplicate their efforts.

What I offer here is practical shoptalk for armchair consumption—in effect, an informal 3-hour refresher course, with the emphasis on refreshment. The book is primarily geared to those writers who've already been through the textbook mill and who now find themselves hungering for helpful tips, inspiration, and a clear, lively synthesis of the essentials. But precisely because it concentrates on fundamentals, the book may also prove useful to the less advanced writer in need of a quick overview of the terrain he's now painfully traversing. I hope so, anyway.

Two last points and then I'm done. First, while you will inevitably find some chapters more pertinent than others, I urge you to read them in sequence, for they move sequentially, not only building on earlier ideas but also becoming more deliberately provocative. The second point concerns chapter 12, Punctuation. It's unseemly for an author to recommend one of his own chapters, but here I feel I must breach decorum, for I know that *no one* is going to read about punctuation, the most tedious of subjects, without special urging. So why bother now? Because chapter 12 is where most of the jokes are (not mine mainly, but others'), and I would hate to be the only person chuckling over them.

Acknowledgments

It's humbling to sit down and inventory your debts after writing a book such as this. You suddenly realize how much you owe to others, and how much poorer the book would have been had you been forced to go it alone.

I owe, first of all, an enormous debt to my students, many of whom read the manuscript at its various stages of development, generously lent me examples from their papers, reminded me in their own writing of what makes for readable prose, and kept me from falling too often into over-solemnity. This is, in a very real sense, as much their book as mine, so strongly did they influence its conception and spirit. Thank you, lovely people.

Of my colleagues at The University of Texas, Professors Maxine Hairston, W. R. Keast, Neil Nakadate, John Velz, and John Walter have been particularly helpful—especially Rea Keast, whose suggestions on organization and whose meticulous editing of chapter 13 were invaluable.

I was also fortunate in being assisted by a veritable brain trust of anonymous prepublication reviewers. I wish I could thank them by name for their wonderful helpfulness and good will—all this toward a complete stranger, no less. When they see the number of their suggestions that I've incorporated into the final version, they will know the extent of my indebtedness to them.

Finally, my thanks to two outstanding people at Prentice-Hall: Bill Oliver, English Editor and resident benign spirit, who shepherded the manuscript these many months with the devotion of a co-author; and Carolyn Davidson, Production Editor, whose literary expertise, thoroughness, and taste made her downright indispensable.

What blemishes remain in the book after all this help are naturally mine only, for here and there I perversely chose to follow my own Muse.

Writing with style

Fundamentals

1 *Getting launched*

Writing and rewriting are a constant search for what it is one is saying.
JOHN UPDIKE

The great enemy of clear language is insincerity. When there is a gap between one's real and one's declared aims, one turns, as it were instinctively, to long words and exhausted idioms, like a cuttlefish squirting out ink.
GEORGE ORWELL

Books on writing tend to be windy, boring, and impractical. I intend this one to be different—short, fun, and genuinely useful.

My chief goal is to take the mystery out of how skilled writers actually think so that you can begin thinking like them yourself. With good thinking comes good writing, as you will see; without it, no amount of technical expertise will save you. Beyond that, this book is essentially a storehouse of practical tips on how to make your prose more readable. You'll find literally dozens of tips in the chapters ahead—tips covering everything from opening strategies to the artful use of semicolons.

For all of these tips to be of value to you, though, you have to start out with confidence in your ability to get a piece of writing launched. What good are the fine points if you can't even get underway? Basic confidence, I think, depends on two things: having a reliable means of coming up with ideas plus some technique of readily converting them into coherent prose. I want to begin, then, where you begin yourself—with the launching process. I want to equip you with a method of generating ideas and getting them down on paper.

But first a word of explanation. It's generally recognized that most people have highly individualized ways of getting their thoughts down on paper. Writers themselves, at least, recognize this, even if the authors of writing manuals tend to ignore it. Some writers love outlines; others gag over them. Some writers dash off their drafts at high speed; others, known in the trade as "bleeders," tend to be mentally constipated or perfectionistic, and refuse to budge from one sentence to the next until the first has been rigorously revised. Some writers spend the bulk of their time lavishly researching their subject; others spend the bulk of their time revising and doing their research after the fact, so to speak. In the face of such diverse methods of composition, I am leery of recommending any one method as ideal, for the question always becomes, "Ideal for whom?" Each of us finally does the job in the way that best suits his temperament. Still, most of us are desperate enough to be always on the lookout for promising alternative ways, elements of which we might later decide to incorporate into our own habitual method. This explains why I'm brashly going ahead to describe yet another "ideal" method in items #3–9 below. Even if you find only two or three features to be of practical value to you, this discussion will have served its purpose.

Recommendations

1 My first recommendation is so simple as to seem puerile, but I can't recall a piece of good prose that didn't reflect it so I am persuaded that it deserves top billing. The recommendation is this: Pick a subject that *means* something to you, emotionally as well as intellectually. As in romancing, so in writing: you're most effective when your heart is in it. If you can't say of your topic, "Now *this* is something I really think is important," you're a fool to write on it, and you really don't need me to tell you. Make yourself a cup of coffee and give yourself a few more minutes to ponder what you would genuinely enjoy tangling with. Eventually you'll come up with a subject, or a new angle of the old subject, that ignites your interest.

If you feel in good spirits, you might consider writing what's called an "appreciation"—of a person, an event, a character, a book, a locale, or whatever. Share your sense of his or its magic; let yourself sing. If, on the other hand, you feel in a negative mood, you might consider writing a salty denunciation after the model of Mark Twain or H. L. Mencken. But whatever you do, *turn your feelings to account*—work in harmony with them and actively tap them. If you ignore your real feelings, which is perilously easy to do, or if you try to write with just your head, the inevitable result will be phony, bloodless prose. Also, the labor of writing will be excruciating. You'll have the nagging, wearying sense that you are simply practicing an intellectual minuet.

But all this is too abstract. We need examples—models of prose that crackles with emotional electricity. A fount of such examples is Pauline Kael, celebrated film critic for *The New Yorker*. Ms. Kael is one writer who never fails to turn her feelings to account. She is that rare creature: someone who thinks passionately. Her reviews —always gutty and dead honest—virtually smoke with emotion. Two brief excerpts will illustrate the point and perhaps induce you to read the book in which she's now collected them, *Deeper Into Movies*. The first, an "appreciation," lovingly eulogizes Marlon Brando's Oscar-winning performance in *The Godfather*. The second is one of Kael's patented 500-pound bombs, this one dropped on *The French Connection*. My apologies to her for wrenching the paragraphs out of context:

Brando's acting has mellowed in recent years; it is less immediately exciting than it used to be, because there's not the sudden, violent discharge of emotion. His effects are subtler, less showy, and he gives himself over to the material. He appears to have worked his way beyond the self-parody that was turning him into a comic, and that sometimes left the other performers dangling and laid bare the script. He has not acquired the polish of most famous actors; just the opposite —less mannered as he grows older, he seems to draw directly from life, and from himself. His Don is a primitive sacred monster, and the more powerful because he suggests not the strapping sacred monsters of movies (like Anthony Quinn) but actual ones—those old men who carry never-ending grudges and ancient hatreds inside a frail frame, those monsters who remember minute details of old business deals when they can no longer tie their shoelaces. No one has aged better on camera than Brando; he gradually takes Don Vito to the close of his life, when he moves into the sunshine world, a sleepy monster, near to innocence again. The character is all echoes and shadings, and no noise; his strength is in that armor of quiet. Brando has lent Don Vito some of his own mysterious, courtly reserve: the character is not explained; we simply assent to him and believe that, yes, he could become a king of the underworld. Brando doesn't dominate the movie, yet he gives the story the legendary presence needed to raise it above gang warfare to archetypal tribal warfare.

The noise of New York already has us tense. [*The French Connection*] is like an aggravated case of New York: it raises this noise level to produce the kind of painful tension that is usually described as almost unbearable suspense. But it's the same kind of suspense you feel when someone outside your window keeps pushing down on the car horn and you think the blaring sound is going to drive you out of your skull. This horn routine is, in fact, what the cop does throughout the longest chase sequence. The movie's suspense is magnified by the sheer pounding abrasiveness of its means; you don't have to be an artist or be original or ingenious to work on the raw nerves of an audience this way—you just have to be smart and brutal. The high-pressure methods that one could possibly accept in *Z* because they were tools used to show the audience how a Fascist conspiracy works are used as ends in themselves. Despite the dubious methods, the purpose of the brutality in *Z* was moral—it was to make you hate brutality. Here you love it, you wait for it—that's all there is. I know that there are many people —and very intelligent people, too—who love this kind of fast-action movie, who say that this is what movies do best and that this is what they really want when they go to a movie. Probably many of them would agree with everything I've said but will still love the movie. Well, it's not what I want, and the fact that Friedkin has done a sensational job of direction just makes that clearer. It's not what I want not because it fails (it doesn't fail) but because of what it is. It is, I think, what we once feared mass entertainment might become: jolts for jocks. There's nothing in the movie that you can enjoy thinking over afterward—nothing especially clever except the timing of the subway-door-and-umbrella sequence. Every other effect in the movie—even the climactic car-versus-runaway-elevated train chase— is achieved by noise, speed, and brutality.

To summarize: It is impossible to write vigorous prose like this unless vigorous emotion is present to energize your ideas, so pick a subject that you have an emotional stake in and write about it just as honestly as you know how. Even if the essay you finally come up with has serious faults, they are likely to seem pardonable. Most readers are inclined to forgive much when they encounter prose that breathes feeling and honest conviction—the reason being, of course, that they so rarely encounter it.

2   Once you've chosen your general subject, take pains to *delimit* it so that its size is manageable. A small garden, well manicured and easily tended, is far more attractive than a large garden that shows signs of having gotten out of hand. So, too, with essays.

You'll delimit your subject in part simply by deciding how you wish to treat it. You might decide that it would be interesting to compare *X* with *Y*, for example, or *X* with two other things. But there are plenty of other possibilities, too. You might contrast *X* and *Y*, or compare and contrast them, or define the essential features of *X*, or explain its implications, or perhaps give several notable examples of it.

3   After you have decided on a promising subject and think you know what you want to do with it—you'll know for sure only later— you would be wise to follow the example of virtually every professional writer: begin like a miser to *stockpile data.* Your data should include facts, ideas, significant details, apt quotations, parallels, and impressions—but principally *facts,* because readers like to be *taught,* and they invariably prefer the concrete to the abstract. Facts are important to you, too. You know from experience that your best writing occurs when you're confident that you have enough data— particularly enough *solid* data. Confidence and preparation are, practically speaking, almost synonymous. Moral: If you have just enough solid data to work with, you don't have enough. If you have a big surplus of data, you are primed to write.

4   To generate facts and ideas, *formulate a variety of searching questions,* both general and specific, such as a tough examiner might ask—Why? What? How? When? Where?—and bombard your subject with them. As you do, *begin sketching out tentative answers to them* in the form of mini-paragraphs. For this purpose it's best to use 5-by-8-inch slips rather than 8-by-11-inch standard sheets. Being half as large, they are much less threatening and much easier to flip through later. (Note: don't confuse 5-by-8 slips with the smaller 3-by-5 cards. The former are sold in pads; the latter are usually sold in packs and are impractical except for recording bibliographical data.)

Each time you formulate a question, take a fresh slip, write the question at the top, skip a space or two, and jot down whatever ideas occur to you. Use as many slips as you need for each question, but be sure to write out the question at the top of each new slip and number the slips relating to each question to avoid confusion later.

Suppose you are a psychology major who has decided to write an essay explaining the behavior of Martha in Edward Albee's play, *Who's Afraid of Virginia Woolf?* One of your slips might look like this:

How does Martha protect herself from
feeling pain and alienation? (1)

(1) She smothers any recognition of her father's lifelong indifference toward her (see p. 225) by vocally worshipping him — a good example of what psychologists term "reaction formation."

(2) "I pass my life in crummy, totally pointless infidelities," she confesses (p. 189). Two probable reasons: to reassure herself that she is lovable and to discharge her strong masochistic feelings (e.g., "I disgust me," p. 189).

(3) She externalizes that self-contempt — and hides her insecurity — by loudly ridiculing her husband George.

(4) She uses liquor to drown the pain. She's now an alcoholic: George remarks that she "can't get enough" liquor (p. 224).

(5) She fancifully invents a child — a son — to bring beauty and meaning into her barren life. The son is one person who is all her own, to use as she wishes: to love and be loved by.

Note that each of the five points could be developed further in later slips and eventually become a separate paragraph of your essay.

Keep at it until you have formulated and framed answers to perhaps ten significant questions. Then collect the slips like cards in a pack and mull them over leisurely. As you reread them, keep shuffling the sequence of questions so that your mind is forced to confront different combinations of ideas. From these different combinations you'll find that unexpected contrasts and similarities will emerge.

These, too, you should jot down, along with whatever new significant details and apt quotations suddenly swim into your brain. Remember, your object is to accumulate data. Data function like fuel for the brain. The more fuel you supply, the hotter and easier it will burn.

This system of pre-writing, you'll discover, has two major virtues. One is psychological: it enables you to write much of your paper before you begin formally writing it. By writing under the guise of merely doing something else (i.e., gathering data), you aren't so likely to choke. The other major virtue is organizational: you have convenient places to store your ideas plus an easy means of retrieving and arranging them.

5   The next step is to decide which of your ideas is the meatiest, the most comprehensive. What you want at this point is an idea that will serve as the *provisional organizing principle* of your essay—something that has at least the appearance of a solid *thesis* (argument). You won't know how truly solid it is until you try it out, of course, but you have to start with something, so get that provisional organizing principle and then sift through your remaining ideas to find an interesting, logical direction for the essay to take. Think of your essay as if it were to be a *story*, which in a sense it will be. Try to imagine for it a distinct beginning, middle, and end.

6   Now that your mind is properly primed, you are ready to start writing a rough draft. Instead of writing a single rough draft, which is what most novices do, I strongly recommend that you *scribble off two or three quick rough drafts* in the same amount of time it would normally take you to write one good draft. You'll find—if you just once let yourself try this—that you'll end up with much better results plus far fewer headaches.

It helps to view the first of these drafts as a mere warm-up exercise; a throw-away effort designed to loosen you up and help you understand better what you are trying to say. Most of it will probably be garbage, even with the pre-writing that you've done, but that's to be expected. Ideas that look good initially have an unhappy habit of looking irrelevant or incomplete from hindsight—and this is as true of slowly composed drafts as it is of quick ones. The reason is simple: you really don't know what you've got until you have established a "position of elevation," as English professor and author Peter Elbow has termed it, and the only way to do that is to get a complete draft down on paper. Novelist James A. Michener put it well: "You write the first draft really to see how it's going to come out."

Here's how to write that warm-up draft. Take one last, leisurely look at your 5-by-8 slips, get a reasonably clear sense of what it is you think you want to say, then resolutely put the slips out of sight and begin *talking* out your thoughts on paper as if you were explaining a concept to a friend. Imagine that he has just said to you, "Now let me hear *your* understanding of it," and you are replying.

Begin anywhere. (The beginning will change later anyway; it always does, even with gifted writers.) *I recommend that you use the same starting formula for each initial draft.* Simply write the words "Well, it seems to me that—" and go from there. You'd also be well advised to put a watch in front of you and set yourself an arbitrary time limit—say, 30 minutes. This will force you to scribble freely instead of compose.

Never let yourself pause more than briefly between sentences, and *don't censor your thoughts.* Just let them come out as they want to— they're all tentative anyway. The key thing is to get them down and keep your mind moving. After a couple of paragraphs of horrible babbling you'll find yourself starting to make sense. Even then, of course, you can count on running into new mental logjams now and again, but don't panic. Simply force your pen to nakedly record all the confusion and inarticulateness you're feeling. (For example: "I seemed to have stalled out here. The words don't want to come. Where on earth can I go with this point?") One of three things will happen: the problem will gradually work itself out merely through the act of verbalizing it, or you'll stumble upon an important new insight, or you'll discover something about your argument that you really need to know—for instance, that it just doesn't hold up in its present shape. A final point: use your own voice, your own conversational idiom, not the puffed language of academe. If you start reaching for fancy language, you'll defeat the whole purpose of this warm-up exercise.

7 Once you've finished, take 10 or 15 minutes to read the draft critically. See whether you still like your thesis, or even believe it anymore. Consider how you might enrich it. Determine which ideas look good and which look extraneous or fuzzy. Ask yourself whether one of those good ideas might be the embryo of a still stronger thesis than your original one. Underline phrases that please you. Try to find places in your argument that need further support. Then go back to your 5-by-8 slips and mull them over again. Check off points that you've made in the paper and underline points that you need to incorporate: these you should file away mentally for the next draft.

8 Now you are ready to begin again. Follow the same procedure outlined in item #6. Put the first draft and your 5-by-8 slips out of sight and let yourself write a whole new version. This time allot yourself 45 minutes. Take care that you don't start slowing up, for rapid writing encourages the mind to function freely. Remember, many of your best ideas are probably lurking in your unconscious. If you slow down to edit what you've written, you'll put an airtight lid on those unconscious thoughts and begin experiencing that agonizing "blocked" feeling that we're all familiar with. (Blockage occurs when the creative thought-making process gets short-circuited by the picky critical process. Experience will teach you that the two processes involve different departments of the mind, and that they function best when kept clearly separate from each other.)

9 After you have read through your second draft you'll have a gut feeling as to whether a third rough draft is required. Don't be alarmed if it is—most professional authors regularly count on writing half a dozen or more drafts. If a third rough draft isn't required, you're ready to begin writing in earnest: this is the *editing* stage, otherwise known as revising or (to the happy reviser) tinkering. By this point you've clarified what you believe and what you have meant to say; the object now is to find the words that best express it and the organization that gives it greatest coherence.

Perhaps the most sensible place to concentrate your initial energies is the opening paragraph. (See chapter 4 for several tips.) Get it in reasonably good shape, but save the finishing touches for last because the essay is still subject to radical change. Besides, your unconscious will need time to do its valuable work, and it will function best when your attention is elsewhere.

After you've tinkered with the opener, go to work on the other paragraphs. Move the sentences and paragraphs around like blocks. Delete every extraneous idea. Brighten up lackluster phrases. Clarify muddy thoughts. Tighten up their continuity. Convert all unnecessary passive constructions into active ones. Look for unconscious repetitions of the feeble verbs *is* and *are*. Correct lapses in tone. (I'll explain all these matters later in the book.)

Don't forget to read every sentence *aloud*. Your ear will catch much that your tired eye has missed. Cock your ear to the sounds of the phrases, their music or lack of it, their freshness or triteness, their jarring repetitions. Ask yourself whether each sentence is immediately intelligible, and ponder the ways it could possibly be misconstrued. Above all, force yourself to search painstakingly for even small lapses in continuity—"lurches," as they're called. Remember, if your reader once loses you, you may at that moment abruptly lose your reader—for good. He has every right to demand smooth transitions between your thoughts, and every right to tune you out if he doesn't find them. "The way to perfection," wrote essayist Walter Pater, "is through a series of disgusts." Let those disgusts be yours, not the reader's.

2   *Thinking well*

The indispensable characteristic of a good writer is a style marked by lucidity.
HEMINGWAY

*And how is clarity to be achieved? Mainly by taking trouble; and by writing
to serve people rather than to impress them.*
F. L. LUCAS

Chapter 1 was meant to serve the function of an emergency first-
aid clinic. Here, though, is where the book really begins, and this
chapter is the heart of it.

I have come to the conclusion that the majority of writing problems
I encounter in student papers should not be considered problems so
much as *symptoms*. I reached this conclusion after observing how
miraculously most of them disappeared after one genuine problem
had been treated: the failure to think well. Thinking well, in this
case, means thinking the way a skilled writer thinks.

Each profession, it would seem, has its own style of thought that
must be mastered before one is at home in it. The law certainly does,
and surely architecture; and so, too, with accounting, merchandizing,
film directing, psychology, carpentry—you name it, they all have a
style of thought related to the nature of the profession. It stands to
reason that writing has its own, too. And it does.

What a novice needs more than anything, then, is to plug into the
brain of an experienced writer—to understand the assumptions he
typically makes, the silent monolog that is occupying his head as he
composes, the special effects he is trying to achieve. Without that
guiding instinct, writing will remain for him all hit-or-miss—a frustrat-
ing repetition of trial and error, trial and error, over and over again.

13

A beginning chess player faces many of the same problems. Lacking any kind of "chess sense," he sits bewildered at the board, moving first a pawn, then a bishop, then—why not?—his queen, all at random, hoping that something good will come of it but knowing that if it does, it will be a mere piece of luck. He simply has no idea how an experienced player thinks at the board. Even watching one sitting across from him, he cannot fathom what the person is trying to accomplish with a particular move, what blunders he's trying to avoid, what alternate game strategies he might be considering. He can certainly appreciate the effects, but the actual thought process is a mystery.

Unfortunately, the grandmasters have made it far easier for the chess novice to acquire chess sense than authors have made it for the writing novice to acquire its literary equivalent. They've published book after book explaining how to think well—what opening gambits to consider, what counterattacks work well, what endgame tactics to employ, and so on. Writing texts, on the other hand, tend to stress mechanics, perhaps assuming that people either know how to think or they don't. Very few books try seriously to explain the psychology of writing; very few focus on strategy and how skilled writers actually think.

I'm going to try to repair that neglect. My chief aim, both in this chapter and throughout the book, is to help you develop what we might call "writer's sense." Very shortly, I think you'll find it as indispensable as radar to a pilot, for it will serve you as a kind of intuitive guide adaptable to any number of unique writing situations. I'll begin by explaining how a novice writer typically thinks so that when I move on shortly to explain how the veteran thinks, you'll have a more vivid sense of the contrast.

The novice

Most of the novice's difficulties start with the simple fact that the paper he writes on is mute. Because it never talks back to him, and because he's concentrating so intently on coming up with ideas, he readily forgets—unlike the veteran—that another human being will eventually be trying to make sense of what he's saying. Unfortunately, his problems are deeply compounded by his tendency to be self-oriented. The result is this: *his natural tendency as a writer is to think primarily of himself and thus to write primarily for himself.* Here, in a nutshell, lies the ultimate reason for most bad writing; it is this natural tendency that he must overcome before he can begin to think right.

He isn't aware of his egocentrism, of course, but all the symptoms of his root problem are there: he thinks through an idea only until it's passably clear to him, since for his purposes it needn't be any clearer; he dispenses with neat transitions because it's enough that he knows in his own mind how the ideas connect; he uses a private system—or no system—of punctuation; he doesn't trouble to define his terms because he knows perfectly well what he means by them; he scarcely bothers to vary his sentence structure through page after page; he paragraphs whenever the mood happens to strike him; he ends his essay abruptly when he decides he's had enough; he neglects to proofread the final job because the writing is over. Given his complete self-orientation, it's no wonder that he fails repeatedly as a writer. Actually, he's not writing at all; he's merely communing privately with himself—that is, simply putting thoughts down on paper.

I call this "unconscious writing." The unconscious writer is analogous to a person who turns his chair away from his listener, mumbles at length to the wall, and then abruptly heads for the door without so much as a backward glance.

Basically, all it takes to begin moving from unconscious writing to genuine writing is a few moments' reflection on what the writing/reading process ideally involves. Think about it. What it involves is one person earnestly attempting to communicate with another. Implicitly, then, it involves the reader every bit as much as the writer, *since the success of the communication depends solely on how the reader receives it.* Also, since more than one person is involved, and since all people have feelings, *it has to be as subject to the basic rules of good manners as any human relationship.* The writer who is fully aware of these implications—the conscious writer—resembles a person who companionably faces his listener and tries his level best to communicate with him, hopefully even persuade and charm him in the process, and who eventually bids him a genial, courteous farewell.

The big breakthrough for the novice writer, then, will occur at the moment he begins to comprehend the social implications of what he's doing. Far from writing in a vacuum, he is conversing, in a very real sense, with another human being, just as I am conversing right now with you, even though that person—like you—may be hours, or days, or even years away from him in time. This break-through is comparable to an infant's dawning realization that a world exists beyond himself.

Actually, since the novice is as much a self-oriented newcomer to his social world as the infant is to his, we might suspect that the simi-larity doesn't end there. And we're right—it doesn't. Both of them pass through a gradual process of socialization and deepening aware-ness. The writer, for example, after realizing that a world—a reader —exists out there beyond himself, slowly goes on to develop an awareness of himself from the reader's vantage point (*objectivity*); next, a capacity to put himself imaginatively in the mind of the reader (*empathy*); and finally, an appreciation of the reader's rights and feelings (*courtesy*). You can see that the young writer is essentially retracing, in a new context, the same psychic journey he traveled as a child. Even the net result is comparable. Having passed the last stage of courtesy as a child, he achieved the mark of a truly civilized person, "social sensitivity"; when he passes the same stage as a writer, he achieves the mark of a truly civilized author, a "readable" style.

The veteran

The thinking process of a skilled writer is directly determined by how he conceives the writing situation. Let's start, then, by develop-ing a realistic understanding of what that situation involves.

All writing is communication. But most writing seeks to go be-yond communication. It hopes to make the reader react in certain ways—with pleased smiles, nods of assent, stabs of pathos, or what-ever. So we can say, generally, that writing is the art of creating de-sired effects.

Now for an essay writer, the chief desired effect is persuasion. Thus, for him, writing really boils down to *the art of selling the reader*.* Suppose you are that essay writer. You want the reader to

* I have misgivings about this commercial metaphor, with its slang connota-

buy two things: your ideas and you, their source. That is, you want him to view your ideas as sound and interesting, and you want him to view you as intelligent, informed, credible, and companionable. (All of these things, of course, are desired effects.) If you don't persuade him to accept you, their advocate, it's doubtful that you'll persuade him to buy the ideas you're trying to sell him. We buy from salesmen we like and trust—it's human nature.

The question we must answer, then, is this: How do you sell your reader? There are four obvious essentials:

1   Have something to say that's really worth his attention.
2   Be sold on its validity and importance yourself so that you can sell it with conviction.
3   Furnish strong arguments that are well supported with concrete proof: facts, examples, and quotations from authorities.
4   Use language that sells—vigorous verbs, strong nouns, and confidently assertive phrasing.

That looks like a pretty complete recipe for successful writing. It isn't, though. Even if we exclude sheer artfulness, one thing is still missing. Unfortunately, it's almost invariably missing. The ultimate way you sell your reader is by courteously *serving* him—that is, satisfying his needs. An experienced writer knows that to serve well is to sell well; equally, to sell well is to serve well. They are complementary activities. The means are inseparable from the ends.

Why is serving the reader so important? Because the writer, for all practical purposes, does not exist without the assent of his reader. The reader has the power to shut him off at whim. This humbling fact of life makes pleasing the reader of fundamental importance, and that's only fair. If you're going to ask the reader to give you his time

---

tions of cheating and duping. Some readers may assume from it that I view writing as a species of Madison Avenue huckstering, where the means are often as unethical as the ends. I don't, of course. Indeed, one of the major themes running through this book is the importance of writing simply, with deep conviction and unaffected straightforwardness. (Note, for example, the Orwell epigraph which opens chapter 1.) So why use the metaphor at all? Why not simply say "the art of persuading the reader"? Because selling is the more graphic concept, and will enable me to go on to develop the twin principle of *serving* the reader.

and attention, then you're in *his* debt, not the other way around; you must be prepared to repay his kindness with kindness of your own. Beyond pleasing him simply to square debts and keep him reading, though, there's also the practical necessity of pleasing the reader in order to persuade him. Samuel Butler long ago remarked: "We are not won by arguments that we can analyze, but by tone and temper, by the manner which is the man himself." I don't wholly agree with that, but it's certainly close to the truth. A pleasing manner surely makes one's arguments themselves seem pleasing because it cloaks them in an aura of reasonableness.

All of us, I think, grasp these facts of life perfectly well as readers, but most of us manage to forget them as writers. Being unconsciously self-oriented, we think it's enough simply to sell. Experience keeps disproving us, though. The reader will always insist on having his needs looked after, as he has every right to, and if they aren't, he'll say "Enough of you" and toss the piece aside.

How, then, do you serve your reader? First, you must cultivate a psychological sense. You must sensitize yourself to what makes *you* buy—how and why *you* respond, what makes *you* feel well served— and gradually you learn to extend that awareness to your reader. This book, incidentally, is as good a place as any to start sensitizing yourself. As you read along, you ought to be asking yourself such questions as: "Is his style too complex to be readable, or too plain, or is it just right—and why?" "What is his tone, and how does he achieve it?" "Do I like it or don't I?" "Why does he use a semicolon here instead of a period?" "Do I like this two-sentence paragraph?" "What effect does his occasional use of contractions have on me?" A writer eager to improve his psychological sense never simply reads; he reads critically. His mind is always alert to the *manner* as well as the message, for only in this way will he learn what works and why it works, plus what doesn't work and why it doesn't. He's like one musician listening to the chords and phrasing of another. What's good he'll imitate and make his own.

Once you acquire the habit of reading attentively, you'll find that your psychological sense will improve sharply, and with it your tactical sense too. This will have an immediate impact not only on the effectiveness of your writing but on your attitude toward it as well. You'll discover yourself beginning to relish it as a supreme challenge to your powers of salesmanship. At the same time, you'll find yourself becoming increasingly considerate. The reader's needs, not your own, will dominate your thinking. And it will give you pleasure; you'll quickly learn to enjoy the sense of communion, the fellow-feeling it brings, for, as in a friendship, you'll be in warm, imaginative touch with another human being.

All of this brings us to the second prime way of serving the reader —schooling yourself to be *other*-oriented. You try to understand your reader. You actively think of him, identify with him, empathize with him. You try to intuit his needs. You train yourself to think always of *his* convenience, not your own. You treat him exactly as you would wish to be treated, with genuine consideration for his needs and feelings. And you keep reminding yourself, over and over, that good writing is good manners.

There are five specific ways you can serve your reader's needs. Please add them to the list of four essentials of selling that I gave you a minute ago; and as you read them, note how they apply to conversation as well as to writing:

1 Phrase your thoughts clearly so that you're easy to follow.
2 Speak to the point so that you don't waste your reader's time.
3 Anticipate his many questions and responses.
4 Offer him variety and humor to keep him interested.
5 Converse with him in a warm, friendly, open manner instead of pontificating to him like a self-important pedant.

Although I'll be following up on all these points in later chapters, I'd like to expand here on #1, the need for clarity, and #3, the need to anticipate your reader's responses. They will give me an opportunity to explain more concretely the assumptions and actual thought processes of a skilled writer.

Phrase your thoughts clearly

A prose style may be eloquent, lyrical, witty, rhythmical, and fresh as Montana's air, but if it lacks clarity, few readers will stay with it for long. Just as no one enjoys looking at a view, however spectacular, through a mud-streaked window, no one enjoys listening to a symphony of words reduced to mere noise.

Hemingway was right: clarity *is* the indispensable characteristic of good prose. It is the first thing a reader demands, and perhaps the hardest thing for a writer to deliver. It is hard to deliver for two reasons: the individual thoughts must be unambiguous, and, even more challenging, the sequence of those thoughts must be logical. Since the average human mind is not accustomed to thinking in a precise, logical fashion, trying to write clear prose is as fatiguing as water-skiing: you're using muscles that normally get little exercise, and they soon let you know it.

In writing just as in water-skiing, though, progress does come with practice. And it's greatly accelerated by imitating the techniques and attitudes of experts. Clear writers, for instance, vary widely in native intelligence, but they all have several basic attitudes in common:

• They assume that their principal object is to *communicate*. They hope to do more, of course—namely, persuade and give pleasure—but they know that communication must come first if these other effects are ever to be achieved.

• They assume, with a pessimism born of experience, that whatever isn't plainly stated the reader will invariably misconstrue. They keep in mind that he is, after all, a perfect stranger to their garden of ingenious ideas. In fact, to him that garden may initially resemble a tangled thicket, if not a tropical rain forest. This being so, their job as writer is to guide him through, step by step, so that the experience will be quick and memorable. This involves alertly anticipating his moments of confusion and periodically giving him an explanation of where he's headed. The Writer's Golden Rule is the same as the Christian's: Do unto others. . . .

• They assume that even their profoundest ideas are capable of being expressed clearly. They aren't so vain as to think that their reflections transcend the powers of language—Shakespeare punctures that fantasy—nor so lazy as to ask their reader to double as a clairvoyant. As novelist Somerset Maugham remarked in *The Summing Up*:

> I have never had much patience with the writers who claim from the reader an effort to understand their meaning. You have only to go

to the great philosophers to see that it is possible to express with lucidity the most subtle reflections. You may find it difficult to understand the thought of Hume, and if you have no philosophical training its implications will doubtless escape you; but no one with any education at all can fail to understand exactly what the meaning of each sentence is.

- They have accepted the grim reality that nine-tenths of all writing is rewriting.
- Perhaps most important of all, they are sticklers for continuity. They link their sentences and paragraphs as meticulously as if they were to face criminal charges in the event of negligence.

But rather than speak for them, perhaps I should let a few clear writers speak for themselves. Here, first, is the distinguished British historian, George M. Trevelyan:

> The idea that histories which are delightful to read must be the work of superficial temperaments, and that a crabbed style betokens a deep thinker or conscientious worker, is the reverse of the truth. What is easy to read has been difficult to write. The labor of writing and rewriting, correcting and recorrecting, is the due exacted by every good book from its author. . . . The easily flowing connection of sentence with sentence and paragraph with paragraph has always been won by the sweat of the brow.

And now novelist James A. Michener:

> I have never thought of myself as a good writer. Anyone who wants reassurance of that should read one of my first drafts. But I'm one of the world's great rewriters.

And finally E. B. White, perhaps America's most respected essayist, whose consistently graceful style entitles him to have the last word:

> The main thing I try to do is write as clearly as I can. Because I have the greatest respect for the reader, and if he's going to the trouble of reading what I've written—I'm a slow reader myself and I guess most

people are—why, the least I can do is make it as easy as possible for him to find out what I'm trying to say, trying to get at. I rewrite a good deal to make it clear.

Anticipate your reader's responses

The chief difficulty with writing is that it's a one-way process. You can't see your reader's face, you can't hear him, you can't get any feedback from him whatsoever. The novice writer, as we have seen, is oblivious to this handicap. The skilled writer, though, is super-sensitive to it; but he overcomes it by actively *imagining* a reader—in fact, imagining many different readers—just as an experienced TV newscaster, looking into the camera's unwinking eye, actively imagines a viewer.

The kind of reader (or readers) that a skilled writer imagines will depend, of course, on the occasion, the kind of piece he's writing, and other such factors. But whatever the occasion, he'll always imagine that the reader has many other interesting things to do with his time, is reading at a fast clip, *and is just waiting for an excuse to tune out.* The writer's challenge, then, is to avoid giving the reader his excuse. The supreme challenge, if more is wanted, is to make the reader forget the other things he was going to do.

How does the writer meet those challenges? Principally by *empathy.* The whole time he's writing, he's constantly switching back and forth from his own mind to the mind of his reader. Like a skilled chess player, he makes a dozen mental moves for every actual one. Each of them he tests with respect to the probable response it will elicit. *Anticipation,* he's learned, is the name of the game. If he can anticipate a response, he has a fair chance of controlling it. So every sentence—every sentence—receives a regular battery of challenges like these:

"Am I droning here? Is he ready to silence me? Is there any way I can lighten this up?"

"How can I get him to see—to *feel*—the urgency of this point?"

"Is the continuity perfect here, or am I allowing fatigue to blind me to a lurch?"

"Is it likely that he'd welcome an analogy here, or is this abstract idea clear enough on its own?"

"Am I treating him as if he were an idiot?"

"Is there any conceivable way that this sentence might confuse him?"

"Have I just used any of these words in the preceding sentences?"

"Will this phrase strike him as pretentious? And, honestly, am I really using it only to impress him, or is this the only way I can express the thought cleanly?"

"Will he get the subtle nuance here, or had I better spell it out?"

"How might this offend his feelings?"

"Can he jump on me for verbosity here?"

"Will he hear a strongly conversational, living voice coming through here, or am I beginning to sound like a book?"

He's equally watchful about the way he paragraphs. He remembers all too well the number of times he's encountered whale-like paragraphs that left him sinking under their weight, not to mention those mini-paragraphs that had his eye bouncing crazily down the page. Too much or too little in a paragraph has the same effect: it wears the reader out. This he keeps reminding himself. He's also watchful of the continuity between his paragraphs. "Is the connection perfectly clear?" he asks himself. "Will my reader want an even sturdier bridge between these parts of my argument?" "Is there any conceivable way he can feel disoriented here?"

And so on, and so on. Writing well is a long exercise in second-guessing and empathizing—even a kind of non-neurotic, self-induced paranoia. It puts a premium on social sensitivity, alertness, and simple goodwill. It is, in short, a very complicated business. But, like mountain-climbing, it's also wonderfully challenging. Rewarding, too. When you've genuinely communicated with another person, when you've persuaded him to accept a new viewpoint, and when the whole learning experience has been fun for him because you *made* it fun for him, that's downright satisfying—hell, it's exhilarating.

Some concluding thoughts

1 *Mumbo jumbo* is another word for grunts of the mind. Mumbo jumbo is what comes out in first and second drafts when you are still writing basically for *yourself*—that is, when you are still trying to fathom what you think about a subject. Novelist E. M. Forster expressed the problem well: "How do I know what I think until I see what I say?"

2   Once you've finished writing for yourself and begin to write for your *reader,* your mumbo jumbo will start slowly turning into bona fide prose—i.e., sentences that make sense.

3   If your reader can't get your full meaning on a single reading, however—*and a single reading is all he owes you*—you must face up to the fact that you are still afflicted with residuals of mumbo jumbo.

4   The best remedy for residuals of mumbo jumbo is the same as the best remedy for an acute case of mumbo jumbo: *shorter words* and *shorter sentences.*

5   When you finally think you've finished a piece, reread it twice, first through the eyes of a nonliterary person (for unconscious obscurities) and second through the eyes of your worst enemy (for all other lapses). This tends to have a nicely chilling effect on overheated and underthought prose.

✕ 6   As a last caution, let the piece stand overnight. Then, in the morning, do as the professional author does and share it with a candid friend. Tell him, "I'm interested in seeing this thing *im*proved, not *ap*proved"—and mean it. As reinforcement, it might help both of you if you quote him a remark George Bernard Shaw once made to his friend, actress Ellen Terry. Miss Terry had confessed her reluctance to deface the manuscript of a play he had sent her for criticism. Shaw wrote back to her:

Oh, bother the MSS., mark them as much as you like: what else are they for? Mark everything that strikes you. I may consider a thing fortynine times; but if you consider it, it will be considered 50 times; and a line 50 times considered is 2 per cent better than a line 49 times considered. And it is the final 2 per cent that makes the difference between excellence and mediocrity.

3 *How to write a critical analysis*

A writer's job is sticking his neck out.

The art of writing has for backbone some fierce attachment to an idea.

VIRGINIA WOOLF

Teacher: This first paragraph reads like a plot summary, David, not a critical analysis. And so does this next one. David, you want to be *analyzing*.

David: Well, I thought I *was* analyzing.

Teacher: But you're merely giving the reader the story here.

David: Well, the reader's got to know what happens, doesn't he?

The chances are that you have been in David's shoes yourself. His confusion is typical. He's been hearing the phrase "critical analysis" for years now but it's still just gobbledygook to him. No one has ever bothered to explain to him precisely what it involves. As far as he can figure, the whole business is circular. How, he wants to know, can you analyze a story without discussing the plot? But if you discuss the plot, it seems you're immediately guilty of "plot summary." It's like *Catch-22,* he decides.

Actually it isn't, although it may seem that way. An analogy may help dispel some of the fog surrounding the two terms. The difference between a plot summary and a critical analysis is analogous to the difference between (a) an account of the highlights of the Vietnam War and (b) an explanation of how the United States happened to get into it, why we stayed in it, and what its effects have been on us. A plot summary begins with no thesis or point of view; it merely recapitulates the facts. A critical analysis, on the other hand, *takes a viewpoint and attempts to prove its validity;* its object is to help the reader make better sense of something he is *already* familiar with.

"Something he is *already* familiar with" holds the all-important assumption. If you look again at David's last comment—"Well, the reader's got to know what happens, doesn't he?"—you'll note that he's been operating from a quite different assumption, an assumption of ignorance. From ninth grade onward he was taught: "Never assume that your reader is familiar with your subject." While this may be sound advice to writers of book reports, it's fatal to apprentice critics, not to mention their hapless readers. The critic's job is to *explain and evaluate*—that is, to bring his reader to a *better* understanding of his subject. Plainly, he can't do this if he assumes that his reader is completely ignorant.

Knowing what you can and should assume is not enough, however. You'll still slip into plot summarizing if you neglect to formulate an interesting, gutty thesis. Novelist Sloan Wilson's remark couldn't be more on target: "A writer's job is sticking his neck out." If you don't stick your neck out, your essay won't have a strong thesis; and if it lacks a strong thesis, you'll have nothing to assert, hence nothing to substantiate. Since nothing can come of nothing, your sole recourse will be to summarize large sections of the plot under the guise of "analyzing" it.

If, on the other hand, you muster the courage and perceptiveness to formulate a strong position on your subject, you're already well on the way toward a genuine critical analysis, since you have obliged yourself to offer the careful argumentation required to make your position convincing. This normally entails ranging back and forth through the plot in pursuit of textual evidence. In the process, of course, you'll find yourself drawing on many details of the plot, as Pauline Kael does in the reviews quoted earlier, but unlike the mechanical plot summarizer, you will always be using those details to *demonstrate a point.* In other words, it is their larger significance that always concerns you, not the details for their own sake. They are *illustrations* of something—a recurring pattern, a character trait, or whatever.

David might interrupt here: "OK, I follow you, but how do I come up with that 'genuinely interesting, gutty thesis' you talk about? I always have trouble thinking up things to write about."

Answer: As you read, and later as you prepare to write, get in the habit of thinking in terms of *how* and *why* questions. These are the questions that a critical analysis usually deals with. They are more intrinsically interesting than *what* questions because they are *interpretive* rather than dryly descriptive. But, equally important, they are more likely to stimulate fresh ideas. Here are some examples:

"How is Hamlet like Horatio—and unlike him?"
"Why does Hamlet delay his promised revenge?"
"Why is the play-within-a-play scene pivotal?"
"How does King Claudius win over the enraged Laertes?"

Well-reasoned answers to questions such as these make for exciting reading because they help the reader to see clearly what before he had seen only dimly, if at all. And thinking out answers to such questions makes for exciting writing because it involves discovery.

Another suggestion: Pay close attention to the *form* of the work. One of the chief goals of critical analysis, said the poet W. H. Auden, is to "throw light on the process of artistic 'Making.' "

If the work is a poem, for example, you might begin by analyzing the rhyme scheme and ask yourself how it reinforces the poem's content, thematic movement, etc. Look, too, at the punctuation for what it may reveal. (You may assume that very little is accidental in a poem.) It's also helpful to ponder these three questions:

1 What is the emotional effect of the poem?
2 How does it get its emotional power—that is, how does the poet manage to make us respond the way we do?
3 How does the poem give us a sense of wholeness (i.e., completed emotion or effect)?

If it's a play, begin by paying close attention to the opening scene, which usually strikes many of the major themes. Also, analyze each scene in relation to the scenes immediately preceding and following it. Adjacent scenes frequently point up ironies, significant contrasts, and the like. Further, be alert to repeated words and phrases, stage directions, and characters' names (often symbolic or ironic).

If it's a novel, start by analyzing it in terms of beginning, middle, and end to get a clearer sense of its movement. Ask yourself what each chapter accomplishes. Read closely the initial description of the various characters for clues to their essence, and be alert to verbal signatures in their speeches. Look for repeated words and images. Ponder especially well the final paragraph: what kind of concluding statement does it make?

For further suggestions, you might consult *A Short Guide to Writing About Literature* by Sylvan Barnet and *Writing Themes About Literature* by Edgar Roberts, both in paperback. If you want inspiration as well as instruction, I suggest you go directly to the master critics themselves. I'd recommend, for starters, Pauline Kael's books (there are five, at this writing) and John Mason Brown's superb collection of theater reviews, *Dramatis Personae*. Reading them is like hitching a cross-country ride in Mario Andretti's Ferrari.

One other question concerns tenses. In analyzing works of literature and film, novice writers often employ the past tense. Experienced critics, however, almost invariably use the *present* tense. This is partly because of the force of convention and partly because dramatic characters are considered as "alive" now as when they were first conceived. Thus, say "Hamlet is," not "Hamlet was." The convention usually applies to authors, too: say "Keats observes," not "Keats observed." Here are two exceptions to the rule, though: (1) If you wish to refer to something that occurred earlier than the time span covered by the play or novel, use the *past* tense. Examples: "Hamlet and Horatio were school chums at Wittenberg." "Reared in the aristocratic home of General Gabler, Hedda was taught to value propriety at all costs." (2) If you wish to refer to something that has occurred before the thing you are now discussing but still within the time span of the work, use the *present perfect* tense. Example: "Although Hamlet has declared his readiness to avenge his father's murder, he seems here to betray a strong repugnance to the deed."

In closing, it might be helpful if I take the major points of this chapter and recast them in the form of working assumptions for you:

1 Assume that your basic audience is a well-informed reader, not the ignorant world.

2 Assume that since your reader is already familiar with the text you are discussing, he will be bored with commonplace perceptions—as you yourself would be—and will feel insulted if you retell him the plot.

3 Assume that he prefers reading *arguments* to mere chat, and that he won't really begin reading with interest until he sees you courageously crawling out on an interpretive limb—like this: "*Love Story* will not be the first disgraceful movie that has laid waste the emotions of a vast audience, though it may be one of the most ineptly made of all the lump-and-phlegm hits" (Pauline Kael).

4 Openers

What gets my interest is the sense that a writer is speaking honestly and fully of what he knows well.

WENDELL BERRY

It is in the hard, hard rock-pile labor of seeking to win, hold, or deserve a reader's interest that the pleasant agony of writing again comes in.

JOHN MASON BROWN

Suppose you've just picked up a copy of *Newsweek*. You begin idly leafing through its pages. With your mind on automatic pilot, your eye instinctively checks out the opening paragraph of one article after another, searching hopefully for something to arrest it. Since you're impatient to get to something interesting, you're a bit ruthless. You give each story only four or five sentences to prove itself, and that's all; experience has taught you, though, that that's usually enough. In the space of those four or five sentences your mind makes a number of small, half-conscious calculations. With computer speed, you reach conclusions on most of the following questions:

"Does this story have intrinsic interest to me?"
"Should I bother investing some time now to find out more about the subject?"
"Is the writing clear and easy, or will I have a hard time following what this writer is saying?"
"Does his style show verve, or is he just going through the motions?"
"Does he seem to be well-informed?"
"Do I think I like this writer as a person, or does he put me off by something in his manner?"

So it goes with virtually everything else you read in your daily life. The point is, though, that you as a writer are subject to precisely the

30

same sampling procedure as the authors you read. You, too, will generally be given only four or five sentences to prove that you are worth a hearing. Granted, if you are writing an undergraduate essay, your reader—your instructor—will go on to read the whole piece regardless of its merits; but if you have convinced him in your opener that he isn't interested in what you're selling, you probably will have lost him for good. He's only human, after all. First impressions are usually indelible. Instead of looking for the good, he'll be looking for the weaknesses, if only to justify to himself his initial impression of your essay. Besides, he'll know from experience, like you, that there is a pretty close correlation between the quality of an opener and everything that follows. If, at the very outset, a writer shows himself to be bored with his subject, unwilling to use his imagination, indifferent to his reader, and unclear in his thinking, he's likely to remain that way. But if his opener reveals an enthusiasm for his subject, a fine perceptiveness, a flair for appealing to his reader, and a clear mind, the odds are that he will continue true to form.

Purely from the reader's standpoint, then, your opener is of paramount importance. But it is equally important to you as the writer, for openers have a way of governing how the rest of the piece will be written. A good opener will give you momentum, a sense of confidence, and an extra incentive to make the remaining paragraphs worthy of the first. There's also a very practical explanation, however. A good opener invariably has a good thesis—bold, interesting, clearly focused—and a good thesis tends to argue itself because it has a built-in forward thrust. It's like a good comedy situation: it ignites.

One of the best ways to test the effectiveness of an opener you have written is to check it for directness of approach. An essay, like a house, can be entered by the front door or by the back door. If you could examine the opening paragraphs of a random set of papers, you'd notice that the most skillful writers usually elect the *front-door approach*. They march into their subject with bold directness, obviously eager to share what they think about their subject. Below is an example, from an undergraduate essay on Prince Hal in Shakespeare's *I Henry IV*:*

* In this chapter, and again in the subsequent related chapters on "Middles" and "Closers," the examples I use of student writing all deal with Shakespeare's plays. I elected this policy principally because Shakespeare is our most uni-

Prince Hal is as hard to crack as a walnut. "I know you all," he says of Falstaff & Co. in his soliloquy ending I.ii, but what friend— what reader even—can speak with equal confidence about Hal himself? His true nature seems finally to be as riddling as Hamlet's or Cleopatra's; indeed, he seems at times to be a hybrid of those two characters: infinitely various, theatrical, cunning past man's thought, loving, brutal, equivocal—the list goes on. It's little wonder that Hotspur, so childishly open and simple, often surpasses Hal as the reader's favorite. It's also little wonder that we are hard pressed to decide whether Hal is actually likable or merely admirable.

The less experienced writers, on the other hand, invariably favor the *back-door approach,* the long way in—like this:

In the second scene of the first Act of William Shakespeare's *The First Part of King Henry the Fourth,* Prince Hal presents a soliloquy which serves as a crux of this play. Although this play would appear by the title to tell of King Henry IV, actually the principal character is the King's son, Hal. The play reveals what seems to be a remarkable change in character for the Prince and follows his exploits in a civil war waged against his father. . . .

This opening paragraph—essentially a plot summary—continues for another four sentences. Would you be eager to read on? Would you even be awake to read on?

Upon analysis it's clear why inexperienced writers such as this student usually elect the back-door approach:

• They haven't taken the trouble to formulate a strong thesis, so they have little to argue and hence little reason to come right to the point—for what's the point of coming to the point when you don't *have* a point?

• Because they have little to say, they are afraid of their reader— they know he's apt to see through their bluff. Thus they instinctively delay a confrontation with him as long as is humanly possible (which often means right down to the final period).

• They haven't yet learned to value their reader's time. In fact,

---

versal author, but also for purposes of continuity. I trust that the intrinsic readability of these examples will offset the repetitiousness of the subject matter, but please pass them by if Shakespeare grows tedious to you.

they haven't learned even to *consider* their reader in any systematic way, for they are as yet preoccupied merely with getting ideas down on paper.

• They have a vague notion that they're supposed to be writing for the World, not for a well-informed reader, and even though common sense tells them otherwise, they cling to that notion since it gives them a way of rationalizing flagrant padding. In the opener above, for instance, the student gives us the complete name of the author (instead of simply "Shakespeare"), the unwieldy complete title of the play (instead of simply *I Henry IV*), and the Act and scene laboriously written out (instead of simply "I.ii").

Below is another example of the back-door approach, but this one is more sophisticated, more clever in its adroit use of smokescreen techniques. The writer begins with some cautious reconnoitering of the surrounding terrain—a gambit known as Establishing the Large Critical Overview—but unfortunately discovers only mists and goblins known as Grand Generalizations. This student knows how the thing is supposed to *sound,* certainly, but having zero to say, she must content herself with a lovely, empty gush. The result is an epitome of The Art of Saying Nothing Profoundly:

Shakespeare's *Hamlet,* admired for its poetic style and intriguing characters, has remained a classic for over three centuries. The character of Hamlet is probably one of Shakespeare's most perplexing and most pleasing. He is easily identified with because of his multi-faceted personality and his realistic problems.

When the student came in for a conference, I helped her to read her opener from the reader's viewpoint. It was eye-opening to her. Gradually she began to realize that an essay is only as good as its thesis, that the opening four or five sentences are absolutely crucial psychologically, that a back-door approach is transparently evasive, and that there is no substitute for imagination. She proved to be an apt learner. Her very next paper showed it. Instead of rewriting the piece on Hamlet, which now nauseated her, she decided to start afresh on another character in the play, King Claudius. This is how her new essay began:

He killed his brother. He married his brother's wife. He stole his brother's crown. A cold-hearted murderer, he is described by his brother's ghost as "that incestuous, that adulterate beast" (I.v.42). The bare facts appear to stamp him an utter moral outlaw. Nonetheless, as his soliloquies and anguished asides reveal, no person in *Hamlet* demonstrates so mixed a true nature as Claudius, the newly-made King of Denmark.

Below are some more good openers, all by this student's classmates, most of them written well into the semester after they had begun to discover what makes an opener click. Note in each case the directness of address—the front-door approach. Note, too, the concreteness of detail, the sense that the writers convey of knowing precisely where they are going, and the salesmanship—the verve—evident in the phrasing. I'll quote the first opener in its entirety, but to conserve space I'll quote only the initial sentences of the other two:

In *The Shrew*, the servant is really a lord, and the lord's wife is really a page, and the schoolmaster is really a suitor, and the crazy suitor is really a wise old fox, and the perfect beauty is really a shrew, and the shrew is really a perfect wife, and things are not as they seem. Even the play itself pretends not to be a play by putting on a production within a production. In it, three characters are being duped by this rampant role-playing. By the examples of Sly, Kate, and Bianca, Shakespeare acquaints us with the effects of wealth, love, and power, respectively, and shows how the emergence of an inner (perhaps truer) character can be said to have been tamed. However, the "taming" occurs only as a result of the manipulation of the supposers by the posers. Moreover, while things are not as they seem because of the dual-roled characters, neither does the "taming" suggested by the title ever really take place.

The occult element leavens Shakespeare's works with a pinch of the unknown and an implication that it should remain so. His artful but often annoying ambiguity seldom allows more than a fleeting glimpse at a forbidden terrain before it is bulldozed out of sight by convenient rationales. Several examples of Shakespeare's significant use of the occult immediately come to mind: the witches in *Macbeth*, the antics of Titania and Oberon in *A Midsummer Night's Dream*, the Ghost in *Hamlet*, and the figure of Owen Glendower in *I Henry IV*.

"He that walketh with wise men shall be wise; But the companions of fools shall smart for it." King Solomon's proverb appears reversed in *King Lear* for it is a wise Fool who accompanies and counsels a seemingly foolish king. In the play, the Fool assumes myriad roles—that of teacher, loyal servant, comedian, and often the punitive voice of Lear's own conscience.

So much for examples. Now here are a few tips to run your eye over as you sit down to write your next opener. Keep in mind, as you read them, that openers are hard for *everybody,* and that even a skilled writer will sometimes have to spend as much as a third of his total writing time trying to get his opener into proper shape:

1 Before actually beginning to write, do two things. First, ensure that you have a strong, tightly focused thesis. There's a good way to tell if you have one, but it takes courage. Write on some note paper, "I shall argue that—," and complete the sentence. Now study what you've written. If somebody else's essay were arguing this thesis, would *you* be intrigued by it? Is it complex enough, or controversial enough, to allow for lengthy exposition? Have you really stuck your neck out, or are you merely pussyfooting?

Second, have on hand a list of concrete details and apt quotations, and be prepared to use them. Remember, if you lead off with a succession of abstract generalizations, your reader may impatiently mutter, "Bull," and tune you out. On the other hand, if you lead off with a number of concrete details, your reader is apt to be thinking, "This fellow has really done his homework. What an eye for detail he has!"

2 Like most writers, you may choke at the very thought of beginning, for writing involves squarely confronting one's verbal and mental inadequacies. You may, as a result, find yourself making half a dozen false starts. Should this happen, try doing what a Pulitzer Prize–winning reporter once recommended to me. He said, "Pull yourself back from your desk, take a deep breath, and say to yourself, 'OK, now, what is it I'm *really* trying to say?' Then simply say it—*talk* it. I got that tip from an old hand when I was a cub reporter many years ago. It works."

3 If you follow this procedure and still feel unhappy with your opener, let it stand as is, roughly blocked out, and return to it after you've finished the first rough draft. There's no rule that says you must write every paragraph sequentially. Remember, writing involves discovery. Once the first draft is finished, you'll probably have discovered several points that really belong in your opener.

4 Use the front-door approach. Idle chat is a confession of an empty brain.

5 Use natural, simple prose—the simpler the better. You can come back later and add small touches of elegance if you have a mind to ("punitive" in the *Lear* example above was doubtless just such an after-thought), but initially keep it *simple*. Simple prose is clear prose. And simple prose, if smooth and rhythmical, is readable prose. Let your ideas themselves do the impressing. If they look banal to you, there's only one remedy: rethink them. Don't try to camouflage their weakness with razzle-dazzle rhetoric. You'll razzle-dazzle yourself right into a bog of bull.

6 Make your opener full-bodied. If it's splinter-sized—a mere two or three sentences long—your reader is apt to conclude that you are short on ideas and thus are only going through the motions. Experience will have taught him, as it's probably taught you, that these conclusions are usually justified. (Of course there's always the glorious exception that makes a dictum like this look silly.) On the other hand, if your opener is barn-like, your reader is apt to conclude that you lack any sense of proportion. He'll take one look at it and groan, "Has the author no mercy? Does he think he has to put *everything* in his first paragraph?"

7 Consider occasionally using a dramatically brief initial sentence— say, 4 or 5 words in length. It will compel you to begin with a definite assertion, give your grateful reader a firm handle on the sentences that follow, and offer him the enchantment of surprise. (Most opening sentences seem to run in the neighborhood of 18 words.)

8 If possible, organize your opening paragraph so that the biggest punch—the strongest statement of your thesis—comes at the *end*. (Note the *Shrew* example above.) This particular organization has three advantages: it enables you to build toward a climax, it gives you an easier entry into your next paragraph because of the springboard effect, and it saves you from having to repeat yourself.

5 Middles

My style of writing is chiefly grounded upon an early enthusiasm for [Thomas H.] Huxley, the greatest of all masters of orderly exposition. He taught me the importance of giving to every argument a simple structure.

H. L. MENCKEN

When you begin an essay, you may have clearly in mind exactly what you're supposed to be doing and how best to do it. If so, you're fortunate. Most people don't. The entire concept of essay-writing is fuzzy to them. This chapter is for the bewildered majority: it's an attempt to bring into sharp focus the *what* and the *how* of the business. The *what* part of it I'll explain with the help of an analogy, out of which I'll draw up a concrete checklist of reminders. The *how* of it is rather more complicated because it involves the very process itself. At the risk of putting you to sleep, what I'll do is follow an imaginary advanced student right through the various stages of writing an essay, after which I'll provide you with a model short essay written by an actual student. This will enable you to see what the finished product might look like.

What, you may ask, has all this to do with "middles"? Well, you are going to see that the middle section of an essay is inseparable from the opening, since it consists of the development of the opener's thesis; and you will see that the middle is also inseparable from the process whereby the thesis is arrived at, since it amounts to a coherent retelling of that process.

First, the *what* of it. When you write a term paper, a final examination, or even a lab report, you are engaged in what's elegantly called "expository" writing. Expository writing might be defined as "informative writing." Its primary goal is to *explain*.

37

Implicit in most expository writing, however, is a second goal: to *persuade*. The two goals almost invariably go together since it's hard to explain something—a political issue, a historical event, a novel, a philosophy—without taking a position on it; and once you take a position you naturally want others to accept it as enlightened. That gets you into the realm of reasoning—the realm of persuasion. The whole point, finally, is to have your reader respond with: "Yes, I understand now. You've convinced me."

From this you can see that your situation as an expository writer is closely analogous to that of a prosecuting attorney, society's professional skeptic-persuader. The analogy bears developing, for once you fully grasp it, you will understand the gist of essay writing.

The analogy

Even before the trial actually gets underway, our prosecutor is already about his important first business, which is sizing up the nature of his audience, the rather motley jury (analogous to your *readers*). How sophisticated are they? What are their interests, their prejudices, their intellectual capacities? Are they a solemn bunch, or do they smile at his little witticisms? The answers to these questions will determine the delivery he uses, even to some extent the evidence he chooses for presentation to them. He's lost many decisions in his younger years simply through misjudging the character of the jury, but he's naive no longer. Now he takes this preliminary testing-and-probing period very seriously. (You as a writer, of course, must rely on intuition, the laws of probability, and guesswork, which makes your task more speculative, but certainly no less important.)

Now he's ready to begin. He could spend six months in Florida every year if he could simply announce: "Ladies and gentlemen, the defendant, Sam Smith, is guilty. You can tell it from the mad glint in his eye. The State rests." Unfortunately, the jury will oblige the prosecutor to *prove* Sam Smith's guilt, and only facts plus cogently reasoned argumentation can prove anything. So, he begins by stating the essence of his case (the *thesis*) in carefully formulated language: "The State will prove that the defendant, Sam Smith, with malice aforethought, attempted last March 26th to level City Hall with his

tank." Then the prosecutor spends the bulk of his remaining time
calling forth witnesses (the *evidence*) to prove his case, saving his
star exhibit (the still-smoking tank) for last so that the impact will
be greatest. All the while, though, he is doing a number of equally
important other things: foxily anticipating and defusing the contentions of the defendant's lawyer; demonstrating his own mastery of the
facts of the case; clarifying what's really at issue and what's not; de-
fining his exotic legal terms so that the jury can make sense of them;
supporting each new assertion with a wealth of factual proof; quoting
authorities either to buttress his case or to freshen his eloquence;
underscoring the logical sequence of his evidence; and providing the
spellbound jurors with a running summary of how the pieces of the
case interconnect.

Finally, he makes a closing appeal to the jurors (the *conclusion*)
in which he neatly recapitulates the high points of his case—he knows
they have short memories—and explains in the clearest possible way
why his version of the case is the only one a reasonable person could
accept. He ends on a note of triumph: "And last, ladies and gentlemen, you have Sam Smith's own tank before you, his fingerprints on
its wheel, the plaster of City Hall still clogging its treads, and 'Down
With All Burocrats' blazoned on its sides, with 'bureaucrats' misspelled exactly as Mr. Smith has always misspelled it." The prosecutor has followed the age-old formula of debaters: "Tell 'em what
you're going to tell 'em, tell it to 'em, and then tell 'em what you've
told 'em." * Following this formula has not only made it easy for the
jury to grasp his argument, it has made it almost impossible for them
not to grasp it.

The checklist

As my analogy shows, there are many parallels between the prosecution of a legal case and the prosecution of an essayist's case. In
fact, virtually everything our prosecutor did finds an exact correspondence in successful essay writing. I want to underscore only the major
points, though.

* The formula works, of course, only when it's kept discreetly veiled. The
trick is to follow it without appearing to; otherwise your presentation will sound
mechanical and repetitious.

At the top of the list is *a sure sense of the audience.* If you ignore the special character of your audience—your jury—you might as well not even begin. It would be as unrewarding as to tell a locker-room joke to your grandmother. (I'll go into the question of audience in more detail later.) After a sure sense of audience come five other essentials, which I recommend that you take a moment to memorize. You will find these in virtually every successful essay:

1 A well-defined thesis or position
2 A clear plan of attack
3 Solid evidence
4 Strong continuity of argument
5 A persuasive closing appeal

To understand what each of these elements really involves, let alone to appreciate their importance, you must see them in action, so let's now follow our imaginary advanced student through the various stages of writing an essay. This will give you the added advantage of seeing the kind of preparatory work out of which strong openers and middles are born.

The hypothetical case

Suppose the student's assignment is: "Write a 1500-word essay discussing your views on capital punishment." What position should he take? Well, this particular student thinks he already knows—he happens to be against it*—but since he is now an experienced writer, he resolves to suppress his notions until he has thoroughly researched the subject. It's partly a matter of self-respect: he doesn't want the facts to end up embarrassing his intelligence. In addition, though, he wants his essay to reflect that he has open-mindedly investigated

---

* Before continuing this account, I should point out that the views and arguments I will attribute to the student are "his," not mine. I've never researched the subject of capital punishment myself, so my own views on it are as unformed as they are uninformed. Unfortunately, the poor student is made to suffer the consequences of my ignorance. The whole point of this fictional re-creation, though, is to show how an essay might be generated and structured. The arguments themselves are irrelevant.

the issues—the pros as well as the cons. He knows that if he doesn't actually do this, he won't be able to anticipate and defuse his reader's objections to his contentions—a crucial element in persuasive writing, just as it is in the courtroom.

So he studies the subject, *recording all the evidence* he discovers: examples, statistics, quotations from authorities, arguments. That's step one. Step two is to *organize his facts*. For this he uses lists. Eventually he comes up with a list of about 20 arguments favoring the abolition of capital punishment and another list of 20 arguments favoring its retention. Having done the necessary homework, he now arrives at step three: *weighing* these arguments. This enables him finally to decide which of the two positions is most convincing to him.

Unfortunately, though, that decision is more intuitive and unconscious than it is rational. As a result, while he now has a firm conviction that the case against capital punishment is the stronger one, the actual proof of that position hasn't yet crystallized in his mind. There's the rub. Until he can prove it to himself, using a conscious, coherent line of reasoning, he knows he won't be able to prove it to his reader. The shotgun approach—a blast of unconnected reasons —is out of the question. His essay must be able to say, in effect, "Here's my position, and this is why any sensible person would accept it." Translated into practical terms, this means showing his reader precisely *how* he reached his position, step by step.

So, he goes back once again to his list of arguments. His aim is to work out a blueprint. The arguments are already roughly organized, but now he must *classify them into major groups*—moral reasons, economic reasons, political reasons, legal reasons, etc.—and analyze how they all add up, how they interconnect. This is a crucial part of the writing process, he knows, for his reader will expect the proof of his thesis to be divided into neat, logically developing *stages,* and this is precisely what he is doing now.

A related task, while he's classifying his arguments, is to decide the *sequence* in which to present them. This is a tactical decision. Some of the reasons, he realizes, are clearly more persuasive than others. Should the most persuasive ones all come first, or should he build his arguments from least persuasive to most persuasive, or should he mix them? Or would he be wise to eliminate most of the marginally persuasive reasons and go for quality rather than quantity? He puts himself in the reader's shoes and decides that if *he* were reading this essay cold, he'd be most convinced by quality, not quantity, and also by an increasingly persuasive order of arguments. Such an order would be agreeably climactic.

He's virtually ready to begin writing now. He's got the *arguments* he needs, the *support* for these arguments, the *coherent grouping* of them, and the most *tactical sequence* in which to present them. In addition, during the ordering process he has weeded out all that is either irrelevant or marginally persuasive (he hopes), so that what he is now going to give the reader is a trim digest of his case. One important thing remains, however, and that is to get clear in his mind the *nature of his audience.*

Two years ago it never occurred to him to size up his audience, for two years ago he wasn't writing expressly for his reader; he was writing simply for himself. Now, though, persuasion is vitally important to him, so it's become part of his standard procedure to second-guess his reader's needs, his taste, his level of sophistication. He knows that this will determine, among other things, his choice of *tone* (serious, bantering, ironic, indignant), his *diction* (elegant, informal, tempered, blunt), his *sentence structure* (complex, occasionally complex, simple), and his *mode of argument* (technical, nontechnical, objective, subjective). All these decisions are crucial, for they define the "voice" and posture he thinks are most appropriate for the occasion.

In this case his audience is well defined: it will consist solely of his philosophy professor, Charles Watson, a bright, serious-minded freethinker who is always warning his students, "Be polemical, but also be practical."

With Professor Watson clearly before him in his imagination,* our

* A clarification is necessary here. I am *not* endorsing the gutless practice of "writing for the teacher"—i.e., giving the teacher (or any reader, for that matter) what you presume he wants to hear at the expense of what you yourself genuinely believe. That's an intellectual and moral sell-out. I *am* recommending, though, that the writer remember who his reader is in order to communicate with him in a manner that is likely to be understandable and winning to him. For example, you don't talk to a three-year-old child the way you talk to an adult, although you may be saying essentially the same thing to both. You use language that the child is apt to understand; you work from where his

student finally starts writing. He opens with a brief, fascinating history of capital punishment and its relevance as a social issue. This consumes most of two paragraphs. Then he ends his introduction with a firm position statement:

> This gradual trend toward the abolition of capital punishment reflects a growing awareness that such extreme punishment doesn't make sense. It doesn't make sense economically, it doesn't make sense morally, and it most clearly doesn't make sense pragmatically.

This thesis sentence provides him (and his reader) with an immaculately lucid, simple structure for his essay. It allows him to plunge directly into an explanation of the economic reasons in his very next paragraph:

> Considered from a coldly economic point of view, capital punishment is a waste of human resources. Instead of killing a man, society should take advantage of his ability to work and pay restitution.

The succeeding sentences in this paragraph develop support for that contention—part of the support being an example of a country that has tried this plan successfully. His next paragraph develops other economic reasons buttressing this one, with the strongest reserved for last:

> Nor let us overlook the staggering court costs. With capital punishment, a single, speedy trial is unheard of. Almost invariably a case will be retried repeatedly as the condemned person exhausts every possible appeal and delay.

---

head is, not yours. Similarly, a lawyer doesn't argue a case before a rural jury in the same way he would argue it before the Supreme Court. That's not dishonesty; it's common sense and good manners (consideration). The argument remains the same, but the presentation of it changes to suit the nature of the specific audience.

He ends the section with a succinct summary of his arguments up to that point.

With this stage of his argument completed, he moves on to the next, the moral reasons. These, he knows, are stronger. New paragraph:

> But beyond the mere economics of the issue, capital punishment is a moral outrage. First, it is a basic violation of the Judeo-Christian ethic, the cornerstone of our democratic society.

He supports this contention by quoting authorities such as Jesus, Clarence Darrow, and George Bernard Shaw, all of whom argue that compassion rather than merciless revenge is the most civilized form of justice. (Here he takes the opportunity to counter a probable objection—the Old Testament notion that "an eye for an eye" is just—with the Old Testament commandment superseding it: "Thou shalt not kill.") Then, in a new paragraph, he moves on to his second argument in this group:

> Furthermore, capital punishment—which is essentially a lynch mob by proxy—lowers the standards of public morality. In effect, it encourages barbarism by the state—indeed, it brings society down to the level of a ruthless murderer. Once the state has the power to murder with the grace of the statute book, historically it loses all sense of proportion. We have seen this happen in Great Britain in the 18th century, when even the pettiest crimes were thought fit for punishment at the gallows.

After developing this point, he's ready for his third and strongest moral argument, which he sets off in another new paragraph:

> Finally and most seriously, capital punishment strikes at the very basis of morality itself. Morality rests upon the fact that we are mortals, frail and imperfect in our understanding, not infallible. By contrast, capital punishment presumes that man can set himself up as God, and that juries never make mistakes. The moral presumption in this is surely as great as that of the criminal who takes the life of his victim.

Now he begins his main attack—the pragmatic reasons. With the gusto of Churchill on D-Day he opens a new paragraph:

> Both economically and morally, then, capital punishment simply doesn't make sense. But the most damaging indictment against the practice is pragmatic: it fails to achieve its purpose, which is the deterrence of crime. Now why does it not deter a criminal? Because it rests upon a false assumption: that murder or rape, for example, is committed consciously, is premeditated. But this is patently not the case. Most capital crimes are crimes of passion, committed unthinkingly in the heat of the moment. The criminal never considers punishment.

To support that reasoning, he cites statistics to show that the vast majority of murders are committed within the family, and that states with the death penalty have no lower murder rate than states without it. He also cites once more the example of Great Britain, where public execution of pickpockets did not prevent the spectators from being deprived of their wallets.

Moving to a new paragraph, he next argues:

> So capital punishment doesn't work. But when we try to force it to work, we find that we can't even administer it fairly. First, there is the economic bias: the rich can always pay their way out, while the poor will die. Second, the meting out of the death penalty often depends upon *whom* you kill, for human life is not valued equally.

Here he gives examples of criminals who were executed for killing public figures, while fellow criminals who killed people of lesser renown were paroled in three years.

This brings him to his conclusion. He succinctly recapitulates his chief arguments and draws out the full implications of them, saying, in essence, "Here's what follows if you don't buy these arguments." Then he ends with a sentence neatly summarizing his case:

> The evidence all in, the conclusions are inescapable: economically the proponent of capital punishment is a waster, morally he is a bankrupt, and pragmatically he is a fool.

The model

What follows now is an actual essay written by a student named
Danny Robbins, a college junior at the time. It's a splendid example
of all five points on our earlier checklist, but especially of #2: a clear
plan of attack. This is about as well organized an essay as you are
likely to see. It also illustrates the truth of George Bernard Shaw's
observation: "Effectiveness of assertion is the Alpha and Omega of
style. He who has nothing to assert has no style and can have none:
he who has something to assert will go as far in power of style as its
momentousness and his conviction will carry him."

The Character and Purpose of Caesar

Octavius Caesar in Shakespeare's *Antony and Cleopatra* embodies
all the ideals of ancient Rome. His pursuit of world power at any
cost is consistent with the militaristic, male-oriented society of which
he is a part. The Roman spirit, it seems, is so deeply ingrained
within Caesar that there is absolutely nothing else in the world of
any importance to him besides strength and conquest. In fact, he
seems so one-dimensional a character that he may not be a true
character at all. I think he is merely a symbol—a voice that recurs
in the play not to capture the imagination or make one learn
something about human nature but rather to provide a measuring
stick by which one can calculate change in Mark Antony.

Certainly there are aspects of Caesar's character that cry out for
further development by Shakespeare. He is so young, yet acts so old.
And nowhere does Caesar show the sensitivity, curiosity, or frivolity
one might expect from a 23-year-old. It seems that if Shakespeare
really wanted to make Caesar a provocative character, he could have
done something with these qualities. But he doesn't. It appears that
Caesar is so type-cast, so stereotyped as a Roman, that the reader or
spectator must view him for what he stands for rather than what
happens to him in the play. No matter what the situation, his actions
are perfectly Roman. And in this manner, it appears that his function
is like that of a "constant" in a mathematical equation, a figure of
never-changing value. Antony would be the "variable" in the
equation. He is changed by the passion of Cleopatra, and Caesar's
function is to provide contrast for this. Caesar, then, must not
change. Three instances, covering the entire time span of the play,
bring this out.

In Act I, Caesar criticizes Antony behind his back for the good times Antony has in Egypt. The play has just begun, and Caesar is already telling Lepidus that

> From Alexandria
> This is the news: he fishes, drinks, and wastes
> The lamps of night in revel; is not more manlike
> Than Cleopatra, nor the queen of Ptolemy. . . .
>   You shall find there
> A man who is the abstract of all faults
> That all men follow.
>
>   **(I.4.3–10)**

This is Caesar's very first speech, and in it one finds a 23-year-old man condemning pleasure. Caesar cannot understand why Antony does not take up arms with the triumvirate, why pleasure comes before duty. This opening speech is a clear disclosure of Caesar's personality. But perhaps more importantly Antony's values are being compared to Caesar's. Not only do we see the things that Caesar values—masculinity, work, ambition—but it is significant that Antony is the subject of Caesar's first lines. In the total scope of the play Antony is the "subject" of all of them, whether he is mentioned by name or not.

Then in Act II there is another, more telling, glimpse into Caesar's character. He and Antony are trying to patch their damaged relationship. But Caesar pursues reconciliation in a purely utilitarian manner. He is a Roman first, a friend second. Caesar acts purely as a soldier. And he is concerned with Antony as merely a once-famous soldier who can help him defeat Pompey. Caesar is so wrapped up in his quest for world power that he will sell his sister "whom no brother / Did ever love so dearly" (II.2.150–151) to Antony to get Antony's support. Antony seems to go along with Caesar to appease him for the moment and end the conversation. Nevertheless, the end result is that the shallowness of Caesar's nature is exposed again. He, unlike Antony, shows no regard for the beauty of human relationships. He is concerned only with using people to advance his military goals. The fact that Caesar shows no love or compassion—not even for his sister—highlights the relationship between Antony and Cleopatra.

Caesar acts no differently in the final Act of the play. In fact, he appears more ruthless. After Antony's death, Cleopatra seeks mercy from Caesar. Caesar—who in the war against Antony has just slaughtered many men in his own self-interest—says:

> She [Cleopatra] shall soon know of us . . .
> How honorable and how kindly we
> Determine for her. For Caesar cannot live
> To be ungentle.
>
>   **(V.1.58–61)**

This is, of course, a joke. Caesar has murdered Pompey, Lepidus, and Antony. The "mercy" Caesar plans for Cleopatra is to use her as window-dressing for his conquests. He wants to use her as a public display of his "generous heart." Proculeius lets slip this notion: "let the world see / His nobleness well acted" (V.2.44–45). For the first time Caesar is making an outward show of pity and kindness and, true to his nature, he is sincere about none of it. Furthermore, the sparing of Cleopatra's life has a military purpose—to make him look good in the eyes of his subjects—just like everything else he does.

Thus Caesar's character never changes from beginning to end. He is not to be pitied or even contemplated to any great extent by the audience. Caesar acts simply as a standard by which one can study the effects of Cleopatra's love on Antony. Shakespeare seems to be using Caesar as a symbol of Roman society, a yardstick by which Antony's deviance from Roman ideals can be measured. There is nothing deep or stimulating about the man. His traits are negative and obvious, so obvious that I think Shakespeare made them this way on purpose. Caesar is supposed to be a model Roman, whereas Antony is supposed to be—and is—a richly complex human being.

The model analyzed

To help you consolidate what you've learned so far, I am going to critique this essay in terms of the five-point checklist:

1 *A well-defined thesis or position:* Like our earlier imaginary student, Danny did the necessary headwork before actually beginning to write. All that preparation gives him two enormous advantages: he can write boldly, because he really knows what he knows; and he can set forth his arguments lucidly, because he understands exactly how they interconnect. The opening paragraph illustrates both advantages.

His thesis is clear and deliciously controversial:

I think he is merely a symbol—a voice that recurs in the play not to capture the imagination or make one learn something about human nature but rather to provide a measuring stick by which one can calculate change in Mark Antony.

It's also placed right where it ought to be for greatest effect—at the climactic end of the opening paragraph. He leads into it with *I think,* which primes us for a major assertion (this is the first appearance of *I*) and which also discreetly implies his recognition that the assertion may be considered debatable by the reader. We are to know, in other words, that he isn't arrogantly advancing this notion as a statement of fact, but rather as an opinion. Nonetheless, it is a firmly held opinion, and we admire his courage for stating it so unequivocally. He's not waffling with us; instead, he's boldly crawling out on an interpretive limb, just as I advised you to do in the concluding remarks of chapter 3. The entire opening paragraph, in fact, is refreshingly direct in manner—another example of the front-door approach in action.

2   *A clear plan of attack:* Basically the opening paragraph is asserting three things, each one leading to the next:

A   Caesar embodies the Roman ideal.
B   In fact, he is *nothing* but the Roman ideal—that is, he is one-dimensional, a walking symbol.
C   From *B* we must infer that his dramatic function is to serve as a yardstick by which we can measure the change in his fellow Roman, Mark Antony.

Danny knows that if he can prove points *A* and *B,* he can persuade us that his thesis (*C*) is, at the very least, probably valid.

In the second paragraph, he contents himself largely with amplifying on points *A* and *B* (principally *B*). But when he gives us the sentence, "No matter what the situation, his actions are perfectly Roman," we can feel ourselves being primed to *view* these concrete situations, for there is where the proof obviously lies. And, sure enough, here it comes: "Caesar, then, must not change. Three instances, covering the entire time span of the play, bring this out."

The plan of attack could hardly be more explicit—or more beautifully simple: three major examples, one per paragraph. This is what Mencken had in mind when he spoke of "the importance of giving to every argument a simple structure." Note, too, the fine positioning of this curtain-raising sentence. Like the earlier thesis sentence, it rounds off its paragraph, thus providing its own transition directly into the proof (paragraphs 3–5). Not a word is wasted.

Danny's plan of attack is made even more transparent by the

parallel structure he uses in the opening sentences of each of his three supporting paragraphs:

a "In Act I, Caesar criticizes Antony. . . ."
b "Then in Act II there is another, more telling glimpse. . . ."
c "Caesar acts no differently in the final Act of the play. In fact, he appears more ruthless."

What reader isn't grateful for such clear signposting of the argument? We notice, too, a progression in the persuasiveness of the examples. Each is stronger than the last, thus building toward an intellectually and aesthetically satisfying climax.

3 *Solid evidence:* Danny has chosen representative examples "covering the entire time span of the play." He quietly draws this to our attention to defuse the possible objection that the evidence is stacked (for example, all from the first half of the play). In addition, on four occasions he has quoted actual lines, which greatly enhances the concreteness of the examples. Many students would simply argue by generalization, assuming that the reader will supply the appropriate textual support. Danny properly does the supporting himself. All the reader has to do is read and enjoy.

4 *Strong continuity of argument:* There are no lurches in this essay. Each sentence, each paragraph is hinged on the one that precedes it. Danny was able to achieve this fine continuity because he had a clear plan of attack: he knew what he wanted to say and what he had to prove. When you know precisely where your essay has to go, you can "tell" your argument as simply and coherently as if it were a story, which in a sense it is.

But the continuity is also the result of careful craftsmanship. Note, for instance, all the parallel structuring: the way paragraph 2 repeats the pattern of paragraph 1; the way each of those paragraphs ends with a key sentence; the way paragraphs 3–5 all begin alike; the way the closing paragraph looks back to the opening paragraph, and so forth. We have *patterns* here. They organize the ideas for us; they silently tell us how the pieces of the argument relate to one another.

5 *A persuasive closing appeal:* The final paragraph is a beautiful wrap-up: succinct, bold, and complete enough to gather in all the major points the essay has been making. We feel them now fixed in our memory.

The importance of continuity

What follows is really part of the "Final Tips" section which concludes this chapter, but since it's both lengthy and vitally important, I'm going to discuss it separately.

> *Good writers are sticklers for continuity. They never allow themselves to write a sentence that is not manifestly connected to the ones immediately preceding and following it. They want their prose to flow, and they know that this is the only way to achieve that beautiful effect.*

But how are these connections to be made? The better the writer, the less need he has for mechanical means of connecting his ideas, too many of which tend to clutter an argument. Instead, he relies chiefly on a coherent understanding of what he wants to say, a simple style, the occasional repetition of key words, and the careful use of pronouns such as *this* and *that*. In manner he resembles a master furniture craftsman who uses interlocking tongues and grooves to do the work of nails and screws.

Sometimes, though, a situation will require a more explicit connective—such as when the direction of the argument is turning or when an idea is to be paralleled or contrasted with an earlier idea. In these situations, the writer will call upon a conjunctive adverb or brief transitional phrase to signal the kind of thought that is coming next. This is called "signposting" an argument—my word for it, anyway. Here he has choices within choices. As Rudolf Flesch points out in *The Art of Plain Talk,* some conjunctive adverbs are bookish—that is, used almost exclusively in print—whereas others are conversational and for that reason a bit less stuffy to the ear. In the list below, the bookish ones are followed in parentheses by their conversational equivalents. Keep in mind, though, that the equivalence in each case is approximate, not perfect. Note, too, that the bookish adverbs afford you greater variety *and* greater precision of meaning—which is doubtless why we encounter them more often in books than in conversation:

above all	in particular
accordingly (and so)	instead
admittedly	in summary
again	likewise (and)
also	moreover
besides	more specifically (for example)
but	nevertheless (but)
certainly	nonetheless
consequently (and so)	on the other hand
finally	rather (however, instead)
first	second
for example	similarly
for instance	so
furthermore	still
hence (therefore)	then
however	therefore
in addition (besides, also)	though
in conclusion	thus (therefore, so)
indeed (in fact)	to sum up
in fact	yet

It's a rather overwhelming list, isn't it? (And it's only a partial one at that.) But the sheer number of transitional words indicates, among other things, just how important signposting an argument really is. Continuity doesn't magically happen; it's *created.* The surest way your reader is going to know how your ideas connect is by your telling him. These are the words you tell him with. I suggest you keep the list propped up before you the next few times you write an essay. It will remind you to give your reader the directional signals he needs; it will save you some word-hunting; and (an added bonus) it will suggest an occasional new avenue of thought simply by tempting your mind to explore other directions of argument—a "nevertheless" thought, perhaps, or a "consequently," or a "for example."

Final tips

1 *"Well, what does it finally all add up to?"* This is the reader's invariable question. Your essay is the reply: *"It finally adds up to this, in my opinion. . . ."* Don't begin writing until you have asked yourself the reader's question and understand clearly what your reply is. If your reply contains an original perception, if it's debatable, and if you've been able to state it in one sentence, it's a good thesis. Now go ahead and prove it.

2 Think of yourself as a prosecuting attorney, think of your essay as a case, and think of your reader as a highly skeptical jury.

3 To prove your case, you'll generally have to substantiate several things. The prosecutor, for example, must substantiate that the defendant had a motive, the means, and the opportunity to commit the crime. So, determine what things you must substantiate, classify your evidence according to those things, and then substantiate them, *one at a time.* This is called "dividing up the proof." If you follow this procedure, you'll find that structuring your essay is relatively simple.

4 Signpost your argument every step of the way. If you have three important pieces of evidence to support a particular contention, *tell* your reader so he can understand precisely where you're going. For instance: "Three examples will bear this out. First, the original treaty of 1923. . . ." Similarly, if you have three arguments and if one is stronger than the others, save it for last and *label* it as the strongest. For instance: "Finally and most seriously, capital punishment strikes at the very basis of morality itself."

5 Assertions are fine, but unless you prove them with hard evidence, they remain simply assertions. So, assert, *then support;* assert, *then support;* assert, *then support*—and so on throughout your essay. Remember, examples and facts are the meat of it. They do the actual convincing; they also have their own eloquence.

6 A good paragraph resembles a good essay: it has unity by virtue of being organized around a single major point. Now several examples may be brought in to support that point, and several ideas to qualify it, and several sentences to illuminate its implications, but there's still only a *single major point.* "One main contention per paragraph"—it's a very sensible guideline to follow. If you don't follow it, your points will tend to get lost, and so will your reader.

7   Instead of viewing the opening sentence of each paragraph as a thesis sentence, as you've probably been taught to do, try this: View it as a *bridge sentence* whose prime function is to convey the reader over into the new paragraph. More than one student has remarked to me that that's the single most valuable tip he's carried away from his writing conferences with me. I say this only to underscore the difference it can make in your prose style. Below are a number of paragraph openers from an often-reprinted article by Bergen Evans called "But What's a Dictionary For?" (first published in *The Atlantic Monthly,* May 1962). They will illustrate the bridging technique graphically:

a   What underlines all this sound and fury?

b   So monstrous a discrepancy in evaluation requires us to examine basic principles.

c   Yet wild wails arose.

d   More subtly, but persuasively, it has changed under the influence of mass education and the growth of democracy.

e   And the papers have no choice.

f   And so back to our questions: what's a dictionary for, and how, in 1962, can it best do what it ought to?

g   Even in so settled a matter as spelling, a dictionary cannot always be absolute.

h   Has he been betrayed?

i   Under these circumstances, what is a dictionary to do?

j   An illustration is furnished by an editorial in the Washington *Post* (January 17, 1962).

k   In part, the trouble is due to the fact that there is no standard for standard.

Even out of context, these sentences suggest how skillfully Evans is guiding his reader, building bridges for him, persuading him. The reader never comes to a new paragraph wondering, "Where am I? Is this the Grand Canyon?" To repeat the point I made a few moments ago: Continuity doesn't magically happen; it's *created.*

6 Closers

The most emphatic place in clause or sentence is the end. This is the climax; and, during the momentary pause that follows, that last word continues, as it were, to reverberate in the reader's mind. It has, in fact, the last word. One should therefore think twice about what one puts at a sentence-end.

F. L. LUCAS

What's going on in the mind of a skilled writer as he approaches his final paragraph? Perhaps we can peer inside one and see. Here's a skilled writer now—our capital-punishment student again. He seems strangely altered, though. In fact, he would appear to be preparing for capital punishment himself. His eyes look glazed. I think we're catching him at a very bad moment:

"This is ridiculous—my brain feels like it's turning to mush. Hell, I think I'll just stop here. The piece is virtually done anyway—I've made my main points. Besides, who's going to know the difference?" (Enter Conscience and Common Sense. They begin beating back Fatigue.)

"No, I guess I can't quit yet. Watson wouldn't accept an argument that merely stops. He's going to want to see the thing *end*—he'll want to enjoy a sense of closure. He once said that's a basic aesthetic desire in virtually all of us. 'Every reader wants his final reward . . .'

"Then, of course, there's the matter of what he'll be able to recall. Since *my* memory certainly has its limits, I'm sure his does too . . . Well, if that's the case, the impressions he has of this piece are bound to be strongly conditioned by the last sentences he reads. My opener may have disposed him to read eagerly, and hopefully my middle paragraphs have sustained his interest, but my final paragraph may well be the chief thing he carries away with him. That's certainly the way

55

it is with the last minute of a basketball game, or the last kiss at the door. Hmm. I can see that I've *got* to make it memorable—as powerful as my opener, if I can.

"But I wonder how I should slant it toward him? I suppose, if he's anything like me, by the time he's gotten this far, he'll be tired. He's bound to welcome a final gathering up of my argument in a form that can be grasped with a single effort of mind. This would also leave him feeling that my argument really does hang together. He mustn't have any doubts on that score. I want him utterly convinced.

"But wait a minute—he'll be bored if my closer does nothing but mechanically recapitulate earlier points, and especially if I repeat too much of my earlier phrasing. That would make him feel that I'm merely going through the motions. It would also make him feel that he's stopped learning things. I've got to keep him interested right to the end. I've got to leave him convinced that my mind is still blazing with ideas."

The closer our student finally devises is half-summary, half-conclusion, similar to a prosecutor's closing appeal to the jury. Almost without seeming to, he neatly sums up the high points of his evidence, and explains clearly and simply why his argument is reasonable. He also takes care to point out its important implications, so that the reader will be convinced that the argument is worth serious thought. He makes the whole paragraph relatively self-contained and packed so that it could serve as a pretty fair substitute for the essay itself, as indeed it may in his reader's overworked memory. And he finishes off with a sentence that has such a satisfying air of finality that his last period seems almost superfluous.

For a long paper—say, ten pages or more—this formula for a closer is probably ideal. In fact, it's almost obligatory, since you will have given your reader a volume of ideas to digest. Unless your presentation of them has been unusually coherent, he's apt to be left seeing trees but no forest. He really *needs* a systematic wrap-up.

With shorter papers, though, you should feel free to take liberties with this formula, particularly if your next-to-last paragraph has already gathered up many of the threads of your argument. You certainly don't want to insult your reader's intelligence. There remain, however, three imperatives, no matter how brief your essay:

1 Get your main point (which may be your final point) in sharp focus.

2 Gratify your reader with at least one last new idea.

3 Give your ending emotional impact.

The four closers quoted below satisfy these three imperatives beautifully. All are from short essays written for the same upper-division Shakespeare course, and all deal with the same subject, *King Lear*. This, I should point out, is no coincidence. It wasn't until these students got to their last essay assignment of the semester—on *Lear*— that any of them learned how to write a powerful closer. When you read them, you'll probably find this hard to believe. Each seems the product of a truly natural talent. Appearances deceive, though. What looks so natural is really the effect of repeated practice, careful revision, and considerable reader feedback, not just from me but from their classmates as well. I suspect that a semester spent with Shakespeare also had something to do with it. As you read these closers, remember to read for manner as well as message:

> After his defeat and capture, Lear's transformation of character is complete. To be a prisoner of his daughters should be the most humiliating experience in a king's life, yet we find Lear expressing real happiness. Because he is with Cordelia, the longing for power and loyalty has been replaced with a desire for love and compassion. At last Lear sees a love without price and power. He actually looks forward to being a prisoner with Cordelia:
>
> > Come, let's away to prison.
> > We two alone will sing like birds i' th' cage.
> > When thou dost ask me blessing, I'll kneel down
> > And ask of thee forgiveness. So we'll live,
> > And pray, and sing, and tell old tales, and laugh
> > At gilded butterflies. . . .
> >
> > (V.iii.8–13)
>
> The kind of love that he now wants is the antithesis of the worship that his other daughters promised him. Lear has discovered a human love based on sharing and feeling, and found that it is worth far more than crowns or kingdoms. The tragedy of *King Lear* is that Lear's ideal universe discovers itself in a prison rather than in a kingdom. For when Lear had the power to preserve love he could not see it, and when he had the wisdom to see love he could not preserve it.

So, by a series of occurrences very close to the core of the man, Lear, this king becomes aware of life just as it is lost to him forever. The only non-static character in the play, Lear becomes the tragic one. The tragedy is one like saving a man's life so that he may be executed. But, in that saving, Lear is, if only briefly, whole, magnificent, wise.

Even though Lear changes into a wise, compassionate, and fit ruler, his sorrows begin anew. The sentimentalist's phrase "poetic justice" holds no meaning for Shakespeare. Ruin wrought in the old king's heart and brain is irreparable, and the tornado that whirls him to his doom carries with it the just and the unjust. Lear's little golden pause of peace, when he and Cordelia reunite, followed by the intolerably piercing scene in which he bears her dead body out of prison muttering that they have hanged his "poor fool," shows that even the virtuous suffer—not at the hands of the gods, who are indifferent, but at the claws of beastly humans. In *King Lear*, the consequences of imprudent action were never followed out to a grimmer end.

It seems we can really only speculate as to what Shakespeare is trying to say about life in *King Lear*. There are no religious morals or Elizabethan motifs jumping out at us like handy crutches. Perhaps Shakespeare is trying to convey in Lear an inner human dignity in suffering. Lear, the exalted, suffers with the common. He shares with all of his brothers the ability to suffer. Suffering is *his* bond. His ability to feel the pangs of rejection, defeat, and total disillusionment enables Lear, who has "ever but slenderly known himself," to achieve a spiritual stature in death denied him in life.

You can appreciate from these examples that what F. L. Lucas said about the strategic importance of a sentence-end is equally true of an essay-end—in fact, probably a good deal more true. A weak sentence-end can always be recouped by a strong following sentence; a weak essay-end cannot. Knowing this, many experienced writers take the precaution, during the early drafting stage, of setting aside a couple of choice ideas or phrases for use in their closer. That's a smart policy. Try it next time yourself and see whether you don't agree.

7 Diction

The case for conciseness

Less is more, in prose as in architecture.

In composing, as a general rule, run your pen through every other word you have written; you have no idea what vigor it will give your style.

SYDNEY SMITH

Most of us tend to write as if we were going to be paid a nickel per word. We've been conditioned, I suppose, by theme assignments in school calling for more words than we have ideas. That inevitably gets us in the habit of phrase-stretching—a hard habit to break. Then, too, it's easier to think in long, ready-made phrases, which have the added attraction of sounding elegant. What businessman, for instance, doesn't feel indebted to "please be advised," "thanking you in advance," and "in reference to yours of . . ."?

This habit of thinking in prefab phrases slowly dulls our sensitivity to words as words. It's inevitable. We may hear someone say, "This is where my head is at," and pride ourselves on our recognition that the phrase is slang, but we'll probably not notice that it's also redundant. (What does *at* say that *where* doesn't already say?) If you think in terms of months, you're only half-conscious of days. If you think in terms of phrases, you're only half-conscious of words.

Good writing really begins with a profound respect for words—their precise denotations, their connotations, even their weight and music, if you will. Once you develop a respect for them, you will find yourself developing a passion for seeing them used thriftily. Why use three or four words if one will say the same thing? Why say "in

59

the event that" when you can say "if"? Or "in order to" when you can say "to"? Or "for the reason that" when you can say "since"? Or "one and the same" when you can say "the same"? Why write "He speaks with great bitterness" when you can write "He speaks bitterly"?

This explains why a skilled writer writes as if he were going to be paid a nickel for every word he is somehow able to delete. His prose is almost invariably concise. Every word of every sentence works at maximum efficiency; the total effect is one of notable power, purpose, and speed.

Let's look for a moment at an example of just the opposite kind of prose. Here is a marshmallowish sentence from a fairly representative student paper:

> His bold and brash temper has been replaced by a careful and prudent manner.

When the student came in for a writing conference, I had him stare at this sentence. "What words aren't pulling their weight here?" I asked him. After studying the sentence hard for a minute, he saw that *bold* and *brash* are essentially synonyms here, so he deleted *bold and*. Then he realized that *brash temper* could be replaced by a single strong noun—say, *brashness* or *impetuosity*. (He ultimately chose the latter for its freshness.) Then he saw that *careful and prudent* was redundant, so he struck *careful and*. Finally he went to work on *prudent manner*, trying to get a single strong noun that would parallel *impetuosity* and tighten the contrast he was making. The answer brought a smile, for it was simplicity itself: *prudence*. The revised sentence now looked like this:

> His impetuosity has been replaced by prudence.

The original sentence had 14 words; the revised one has just 7. (It can be revised even further, as I'll show in a moment when I discuss verbs.) There is no question which version has the greater vigor and pleasing directness. Less *is* more. A good writer will perform this kind of operation on every sentence, going back over them again and again, laboriously, even obsessively, until he is satisfied that he cannot make his phrases any more succinct without sacrificing clarity. Hemingway spoke truly: "Writing must be a labor of love or it is not writing."

There's a moral in this story. Perhaps the major difference between a successful writer and an unsuccessful writer is simply this: the successful writer is prepared to take many more pains to say it cleanly. What looks like greater brainpower is usually merely greater persistence. The student demonstrated the point to himself. On that day he became a convert to conciseness and went on to become one of the best writers in his class.

The case for vigorous verbs

Active: The trout *took* the bait.
Passive: The bait *was taken* by the trout.

All of us were taught at one time or another that the active verbal voice is preferable to the passive voice.* Most of us, though, have probably forgotten why—if, in fact, we were ever told why in the first place. And most of us, even while remembering which is the preferred form, tend to overuse the passive voice nonetheless. I want to re-explain here the advantages of using the active voice and also explain our curious habit of overusing the passive voice in spite of ourselves.

Good prose is *direct, definite.* Like a firm handshake, it betokens confidence—and it inspires confidence. It implies to the reader: "You're in good hands with me. I have carefully thought out what I think about this subject and believe it makes sense, so I'm giving it to you just as I see it. I respect you too much to waste your valuable time with vagueness and wordiness, and I respect myself too much to be tempted into pussyfooting. Of course we'll probably disagree with

---

* Quick grammar review: A verb is considered "active" when its subject is the actor doing whatever action the verb is describing. The verb becomes "passive," though, if its subject is being acted upon by something else. In the first sentence of this footnote, "is considered" is a passive construction since its subject, "verb," is the recipient of the action, not the agent of it. (Here the agent is unspecified.) The passive voice, incidentally, is always composed of *is* (or *was,* or *were,* or *has been*) plus a past participle.

one another here and there, but at least we'll both have the satisfaction of knowing precisely where we disagree."

Weak prose, conversely, is *roundabout, vague.* Like a weak handshake, it betokens insecurity. It implies to the reader: "You probably should have chosen a different guide. At heart I'm afraid of you; I'm equally afraid of being me. Even worse, I confess I'm not sure just what I think about this subject, and thus I can't give it to you straight. I can't help but be vague, you see—it's the only refuge I have. It's my smoke screen. Vagueness enables me to get by with half-understanding, and it also disarms you a bit since you'll have difficulty knowing precisely where you disagree with me."

Many elements in a writer's style, as you might expect, contribute to these impressions. Surely one of the chief elements, though, is the writer's choice of verbs. Why? Because the verb, for better or worse, functions as the power center of every sentence. If a writer's verbs are active, genuinely fresh, and definite, his sentences will have snap; they'll inevitably impress us with his spirit and conviction. But if his verbs are passive, drab, and roundabout, the sentences will sag; they'll impress us with his dullness and diffidence. *Because every sentence normally has at least one verb, the aggregate effect of an essay's verbs will necessarily be considerable.*

Theodore Bernstein makes this point very tellingly in his book, *The Careful Writer.* He uses the Declaration of Independence as an example. The authors of that document wanted to do two things: justify the colonists' claims to independence and galvanize them into open rebellion. Both ends they accomplished with superb effect. How? In large part by employing vigorous, unequivocal verbs. Of the 1,500 words in the document, Bernstein points out, only a dozen or so verbs appear in the passive form. The others are notably active like these: "[King George III] has plundered our seas, ravished our Coasts, burned our towns, and destroyed the lives of our people."

Sometimes, to be sure, the passive voice is desirable. For example, you may wish to emphasize the effect of a particular action: "Smith was killed in the accident." Or you may wish to soften the phrasing of an idea: "You would be advised to leave now." Or you may be ignorant of the agent performing the action: "The ransom note was left in the mailbox last night." And sometimes it doesn't matter who performed an action: "That house was rebuilt years ago."

Generally, though, the active voice is preferable. You can prove this for yourself simply by taking an old piece you have written and converting every unnecessarily passive verb into the active form. You'll be astonished at how much this alone invigorates your style. While you're at it, you might perform an allied operation that has a similar effect: recast as many of your colorless *is* and *are* constructions as possible. The feeblest of these tend to be the expletives (*there is, there are, there were*) and the impersonal constructions (*it is, it was*), which allow a writer to get all the way past the subject and verb positions of a sentence without having said a thing. What weight are they pulling? None.

The following examples will illustrate these points. Note in each case the difference in conciseness:

1 His impetuosity *has been replaced* by prudence.
  Prudence now *tempers* his impetuosity.
2 It *is said* that power *is corrupting.*
  Power *corrupts.*
3 Meaning *was found* by Freud in everything.
  Freud *detected* meaning in everything.
4 *There were* two hundred guests *in attendance* at the party.
  Two hundred guests *attended* the party.
5 *It was decided* to destroy the evidence.
  [?] *decided* to destroy the evidence.

The last of these examples illustrates another problem with the passive: it allows the writer to avoid assigning responsibility for an action to a specific agent. Who actually made the decision to destroy the evidence? We aren't told. The buck is passed, the position hedged. The passive voice thus serves as a convenient smoke screen for a person who either lacks specific knowledge of something or has reason to conceal it.

Unfortunately, it's one thing to recognize the superiority of active verbs in a set of examples but quite another thing to act on that awareness in your actual writing. The reason is this: practically speaking, your "choice" of verb forms is seldom an actual choice at all. Rather, it tends to be automatic and not easily changed since the verbal voice you employ is, at bottom, an expression of *attitude*— toward yourself, your reader, and your subject. If you are blessed

with confidence, whether it be innate or earned as a result of knowing you've mastered your subject, you'll almost instinctively employ
the active voice, since it will be natural for you to assert what you
know, and to assert it in bold terms. If, however, you are funda-
mentally insecure about your thesis, you'll almost instinctively turn
to the passive voice as a refuge.

All that granted, the knowledge of how telltale your verbs are can
still be a decided help. It enables you, during the final editing stage
of composition, to spot passages of weak argumentation that you
have been oblivious to earlier. All you have to do is read your essay
once through looking exclusively at your verbs. You ought, in fact,
to get in the habit of doing this with every piece you write. The small
investment of time will pay rich dividends.

The case for freshness

*The difference between the almost right word and the right word is really a
large matter—'tis the difference between the lightning-bug and the lightning.*
MARK TWAIN

"There is no deodorant like success," writes Elizabeth Taylor. We
read that and we stop in our tracks, smiling with amusement, perhaps
even chuckling out loud. What captivates us? The answer is clear:
the perfect freshness and whimsical aptness of the image.

Every time we write we have opportunities to delight our reader
with arresting phrases like that one. Here's another, from the pen of
critic John Aldridge, demolishing a piece of current fiction: "the
drama, which develops at about the speed of creeping crab grass. . . ."
And yet another, by novelist Kurt Vonnegut: "He had an upper-
class Hoosier accent, which sounds like a bandsaw cutting gal-
vanized tin." And one more, this one from T. S. Eliot as he reaches
the end of several paragraphs of highly theoretical speculation: "Have
I been toiling to weave a labored web of useless ingenuity?" Ah!

Each of these authors instinctively understands one of the chief
secrets of artful writing: you must keep the reader in a state of near-
perpetual surprise. Not suspense, but *surprise*. It's like baseball. A
skilled pitcher mixes up his pitches. He'll throw a fast ball, then a
curve, maybe a change-of-pace, then a knuckle ball. Skilled writers

work much the same way. They're constantly feeding the reader's appetite for novelty, be it with a fresh idea, a fresh phrase, or a fresh image. And if they're naturally witty, they'll also serve him up the amusingly off-beat—the literary equivalent of a knuckle ball. Woody Allen's brilliant *New Yorker* pieces, now collected in his book *Getting Even,* provide classic examples of the latter.

I think you might find it instructive to listen to a few professionals talk about their art. The agreement among them is remarkable. Here, first, is master storyteller Theodor Seuss Geisel (Dr. Seuss):

> We throw in as many fresh words as we can get away with. Simple, short sentences don't always work. You have to do tricks with pacing, alternate long sentences with short, to keep it alive and vital. Virtually every page is a cliff-hanger—you've got to force them to turn it.

Now, novelist Ford Madox Ford:

> Carefully examined, a good—an interesting—style will be found to consist in a constant succession of tiny, unobservable surprises.

An anonymous critic reviewing another writer's book:

> Best of all his style is laced with little surprises of diction or structure and the small shocks of well-made metaphors.

Science-fiction writer Ray Bradbury:

> Creativity is continual surprise.

To write creatively—to come up with "a constant succession of tiny surprises"—we must *want* to. We all have imaginations; the trick is to use them. And it's in the using of them that writing suddenly becomes a labor of love—an intensely creative, pleasurable activity. Each time we set down a sentence we must ask ourselves: *"Now how can I express this more memorably?"* Occasionally, the mere addition of a choice adjective is all that is needed:

He wrote with a *surgical* indifference to feelings.—WILLIAM NOLTE

More frequently, an adjustment of the verb—the engine of the sentence—will bring the desired effect:

> A prig is one who delights in demonstrating his superiority on small occasions, and it is precisely when he has a good case that he *rises* to the depths of prigocity.—DWIGHT MACDONALD

(Actually, this last sentence works its magic on us by two surprises, not one—first through the witty substitution of *rises* for *sinks,* and second through the wonderful nonce word *prigocity,* which converts mere priggishness into a complete and seemingly even fussier state of being.) But perhaps the best way, as the earlier examples showed, is through an image—a simile, say, or a metaphor.* Both are pictorial analogies which can explain and delight at the same time.

Unfortunately, memorable analogies seldom come unsought. Usually the writer must actively go out beating the bushes of his imagination to scare them up. A good tip is: *Always be thinking in terms of "like."* Such-and-such is like—like what? Challenge your imagination. What *is* it similar to? Do this with every sentence you write. Make it part of your writing habit. Charles Ferguson, in *Say It with Words,* offers another tip that will help you actually cultivate these metaphors and similes. I confess I was initially dubious as to its value, but after trying it (with some modifications) I found it to be wonderfully fruitful. Here is his recommendation:

> Let a person think, and as far as possible speak, for one day a week in the terms common to some particular profession or trade. In his reflections let him pick images from this vocabulary, and let him by this process see how many can be carried over into common speech and writing. On Monday it might be that he would choose his images from cooking; on Tuesday from engineering; on Wednesday from railroading; on Thursday from nuclear science; on Friday from agriculture; on Saturday from sport. And by Sunday he could

---

* A simile compares two things using *like* or *as* (e.g., "That apartment is like a zoo"); a metaphor makes the comparison without using *like* or *as* (e.g., "That apartment is a zoo").

certainly need a rest, but if he continued the process he might choose his terms from the wealth of language in the field of religion.

Sometimes, when an analogy suggests itself, you can simply tack it right on to the end of your sentence—like this:

> A professor must have a theory, as a dog must have fleas.
> —H. L. MENCKEN

Sometimes you can even frame the entire thought in terms of the comparison: you simply drop the explicit *like* or *as* and develop the analogy metaphorically. Here, for example, is an excerpt from John Mason Brown's review of *Death of a Salesman* which brilliantly illustrates the use—and effect—of a well-chosen metaphor:

> Mr. [Lee J.] Cobb's Willy Loman is irresistibly touching and wonderfully unsparing. He is a great shaggy bison of a man seen at that moment of defeat when he is deserted by the herd and can no longer run with it. Mr. Cobb makes clear the pathetic extent to which the herd has been Willy's life.

The beauty of that metaphor is that it allows us to *see* Cobb's portrayal of Willy Loman. We are given a visual—even an emotional—correlative of the bare abstract idea, and so that idea comes alive to us, and haunts our imagination with its poignance.

You can understand now, I think, why novelist Joseph Conrad could proclaim as his artistic mission: "My task which I am trying to achieve is, by the power of the written word to make you hear, to make you feel—it is, above all, to make you *see*. That—and no more, and it is everything."

Occasionally you run across a passage which seems the very quintessence of fresh, visual writing. Such a one, I believe, is the little vignette below, by novelist John Updike, appearing in his *Assorted Prose*. It makes a fitting conclusion to this chapter, for it says it all— by example. Read it twice, please:

> We recently had a carpenter build a few things in our house in the country. It's an old house, leaning away from the wind a little; its

floors sag gently, like an old mattress. The carpenter turned his back on our tilting walls and took his vertical from a plumb line and his horizontal from a bubble level, and then went to work by the light of these absolutes. Fitting his planks into place took a lot of those long, irregular, oblique cuts with a ripsaw that break an amateur's heart. The bookcase and kitchen counter and cabinet he left behind stand perfectly up-and-down in a cockeyed house. Their rectitude is chastening. For minutes at a stretch, we study them, wondering if perhaps it isn't, after all, the wall that is true and the bookcase that leans. Eventually, we suppose, everything will settle into the comfortably crooked, but it will take years, barring earthquakes, and in the meantime we are annoyed at being made to live with impossible standards.

Note the seeming inevitability of the phrasing, so right is each word. Note, too, the originality of perception, the "small shocks of well-made metaphors," the fine wit (especially the pun on "rectitude"), and the sense of perfect wholeness it achieves. Updike knows how to break an amateur's heart himself.

8   *Tips for increasing your readability*

When we encounter a natural style, we are astonished and delighted; for we expected to see an author, and we find a man.

PASCAL

Sentences are not different enough to hold the attention unless they are dramatic. No ingenuity of varying structure will do. All that can save them is the speaking tone of voice somehow entangled in the words and fastened to the page for the ear of the imagination.

ROBERT FROST

A readable style is a style that invites reading. That circular definition I think we can all agree on. But when we ask what makes a style readable, we move into the subjective arena of personal taste. Here it's strictly each person for himself. I'd like to take a moment to state my views on the subject, for whatever they're worth. If you happen to agree with them, then you might find the tips that follow both sensible and helpful.

Basically, I require two things of an author. The first is that he have something interesting to say—something that will either teach me or amuse me. If he doesn't, I stop reading. The second requirement is that he not waste my time getting out what he has to say. If he idles, I conclude that I can be taught quicker elsewhere.

Beyond these two basic requirements, what I find most appealing in a writer is an authentic personal manner. I like to see him come across as a living, companionable human being, not as an emotional eunuch or stuffed shirt. I like to have an author *talk* to me, unbend to me, speak right out to me. If his prose has a natural, conversational rhythm to it, if it's forged out of basic, idiomatic English rather than pretentious Highbrow English, if it's stamped with the mark of his quirky personality, if it carries the ring of honesty and passionate conviction, then he's my man. What I'm saying, I guess, is that I like an author to be himself, warts and all. It shows me that he trusts me with his vulnerability, isn't afraid of me, and isn't afraid of himself either.

Below is an example of what I mean—an example, too, of what Pascal and Frost doubtless had in mind in the remarks of theirs that I quoted a moment ago. It's the opening paragraph of F. Scott Fitzgerald's celebrated piece, "The Crack-up":

> Of course all life is a process of breaking down, but the blows that do the dramatic side of the work—the big sudden blows that come, or seem to come, from outside—the ones you remember and blame things on and, in moments of weakness, tell your friends about, don't show their effect at once. There is another sort of blow that comes from within—that you don't feel until it's too late to do anything about it, until you realize with finality that in some regard you will never be as good a man again. The first sort of breakage seems to happen quick—the second kind happens almost without your knowing it but is realized suddenly indeed.

What permits such a miracle of literary authenticity to happen? A hard question. The answer, I think, is either a religious reverence for truth at whatever cost—this is proverbially the case with major artists—or else genuine self-acceptance. If a person accepts himself, he will be himself, and will speak his mind in his own idiom without inhibition. He won't be engaged in posturing with his reader, or counterfeiting his real personality and feelings, because he'll have no wobbly idealized self to defend.

Achieving this self-acceptance is a difficult proposition, though. The fear of rejection straitjackets most of us from early in life. Instead of learning to express our real feelings, we learn to disguise them. Instead of learning to discover our own writing voice, we learn to mimic the voice of others. In fact, we do a pretty good job of learning to smother all traces of individuality.

If we're honest with ourselves, most of us can see this defensiveness operating every time we're called upon to produce a piece of serious writing—an esssay, for example, or a report. At such times, fear compels us to try to appear more godlike than we normally are: wiser, more rational, more authoritative. But since, beyond a certain point, we can't become more rational and authoritative, we instinctively— and often quite unconsciously—compensate in our writing style by donning the trappings of pure rationality and authority: studied "objectivity," complete impersonality of address, elevated diction, a grave manner, elaborate sentences, and the rest. It can be pretty convincing. Sometimes we can even fool ourselves with our stylistic majesty.

Unfortunately, this is in great part a learned response. What keeps reinforcing it is the popular dogma that only a lofty, formal style is appropriate in serious writing. That dogma not only strengthens our feeling that we must be something we're not, but also teaches us *how* to strike the godlike pose.

How did the dogma originate? Probably through the accumulation of thousands of precedents resembling our own attempts at imposture. After enough people over enough decades donned the trappings of authority, the trappings themselves inevitably became part of the established style of discourse for serious situations. At that point Decorum—not just the individual's ego—began insisting on a standard of stylistic acceptability. From then until now we have had convention reinforcing instinct, and instinct in turn rigidifying convention—in short, a vicious circle.

You can see it operating at every commencement exercise. A speaker has been chosen to give the major address. "My God, what can I say that will be equal to the occasion?" he privately wails to himself. He thinks and thinks; his desperation grows; his brain begins to freeze. Eventually he bows to tradition and comes up with an impossibly formal Address—a collection of high-flown platitudes substituting for genuine feeling and profundity. The audience hears it, yawns, then dozes. Each person leaves with the same unspoken sentiment: "Well, one more boring commencement speech. Why doesn't someone—just once—give a simple, heartfelt talk, something really honest? Why must it always be so absurdly pretentious?" Because, as we've seen, convention—and the speaker's frightened ego—won't have it any other way. With each new precedent, it becomes all the harder for a new commencement speaker to be simply himself.

The only way to break this circle, I think, is for each of us to subject the dogma of Formalism to a searching analysis. How solid, in fact, is its rationale? What are its actual effects? What (if any) reasonable alternative is there to it? And what are the stylistic practices of our best contemporary authors?

Let's begin with the rationale for Formalism. If we judge it solely on the basis of the corrective ends it's usually meant to serve, we can have no quarrel with it. The teachers who preach the formal style are trying desperately to elevate the writing standards of their students. More specifically, they hope to teach them stylistic discipline and grace; teach them that talking and writing, while related, are not the same thing; teach them, in short, that when one writes seriously, one must take one's style seriously. In essence, they are reacting against the shortcomings of the informal style adopted unthinkingly by their students. Since such a style recognizes no difference between writing and talking, it tends to be loose, banal, and imprecise—disadvantages too great to offset its merits of simplicity and ease.

So far so good. Unfortunately, what these teachers fail to perceive is that the archly conservative formal style which they preach as a corrective has serious shortcomings of its own. While capable of satisfying the needs for precision and conciseness, it tends to lack ease and frequently freshness too, since it inhibits variety of diction, simplicity, and anything offbeat. Its elaborate self-consciousness is both its virtue and its limitation.

This brings me to its actual effects. There are two principal ones, it seems to me, both of them negative. First, more often than not it ironically promotes writing as bad in its own way as the very writing it's hoping to discourage—"bow-wow" language (Mencken called it) marked by stilted diction, highly abstract phraseology, frozen sentence rhythms, and so on. The exceptionally literate person may eventually find himself at home with a formal style, true, but the average writer never will—and his awkwardness will show. Second, and more insidious, it promotes phoniness and empty conventionality—the Standard Way of Thinking, so to speak. When a person is obliged to write like another person, who was himself obliged to write like still another person, he is invariably going to start adopting that person's neutered style of thought and stray further and further from what he himself actually thinks and feels. But that's just the beginning. Teach a person this trick and pretty soon he's formed a lifelong habit. We see the dismaying evidence all around us—in "businesese," "academese," "officialese," "federal prose." Their labels may differ, but not their gobbledygook essence. Each is a form of imitation writing sterile in its uniformity, incomprehensible in its jargon, and absurd in its pomposity. People don't learn to write this way who have been encouraged to write simply, directly, and honestly. They learn to write this way only when they've been taught a style which implies that naturalness is unnatural, that informality is unacceptable, and that individuality is unpardonable. (More on this in the next chapter.)

George Orwell discusses something closely analogous to the syndrome I'm describing in his brilliant essay, "Politics and the English Language." He observes, for instance:

> As I have tried to show, modern writing at its worst does not consist in picking out words for the sake of their meaning and inventing images in order to make the meaning clearer. It consists in gumming together long strips of words which have already been set in order by someone else, and making the results presentable by sheer humbug. . . .
> In our time it is broadly true that political writing is bad writing. Where it is not true, it will generally be found that the writer is some sort of rebel, expressing his private opinions and not a "party line." Orthodoxy, of whatever color, seems to demand a lifeless, imitative style.

That last sentence says it all.

We might solve the problem, it seems to me, if we stop thinking of style in the simplistic either/or terms that the formalists have taught us to adopt. Typifying their way of thinking is the following entry on contractions in one of the most widely used Freshman English texts: "The use of contractions (I'll, can't, couldn't, didn't, he's, shouldn't) is appropriate in informal and colloquial styles but not in a formal style." The trouble with such a dictum is that it postulates only two kinds of style, both of them extreme—an informal, colloquial style vs. a formal style—and implies that only the latter is legitimate for serious writing. What the student is never told is that there exists a *middle* style—"General English," professor Porter Perrin calls it—which is essentially a happy compromise between formal and informal. Being a compromise, it is by far the most palatable of the written styles, and its area of appropriateness—at least in the real world—is virtually unlimited. Why? Because a skilled writer can stay within the "General English" style and still satisfy the four essentials of prose: precision, conciseness, ease, and freshness. (Indeed, as I've shown, he'd be hard put to satisfy all four with any other style.) Little wonder that it has been displacing formal English as the most popular literary style in recent years.

The special character of this style—at least at its best—was caught by novelist Somerset Maugham when he remarked, "good prose should resemble the conversation of a well-bred man." Several illustrations of it appear in this book—most notably the passages by Kael in chapter 1, by White in chapter 2, by Updike in chapter 7, and by Fitzgerald in the present chapter. If you glance again at these passages, you'll observe that each is strikingly conversational in tone—unaffected, idiomatic, straightforward—but at the same time beautifully wrought. The phrasing is tight and precise, the diction fresh and apt. Considerable labor has been lavished on these sentences, we can be sure, and not a little of it has doubtless been spent concealing that labor. They all seem like happy accidents—precisely the intended effect.

What makes such a style so appealing to today's reader is its authenticity and graceful informality. What makes it so attractive to the writer himself, I think, is that it frees him to discover his own voice. Moreover, it reinforces his desire to speak the truth as he sees it. All of us need that reinforcement—we need as much of it as we can get, in fact. We surely don't get it when we feel compelled by a stylistic dogma to efface our personality, adopt the language of orthodoxy, and pretend to an exalted authority we know we don't possess. Bonamy Dobrée, in his *Modern Prose Style,* summed up the matter well:

> The modern prose-writer, in returning to the rhythms of everyday speech, is trying to be more honest with himself than if he used, as is too wreckingly easy, the forms and terms already published as the expression of other people's minds.

Unfortunately, while the "General English" style may be our answer, it doesn't simplify our writing problems. Just the reverse: the more you poke into its subtle complexities, the more you conclude that it's likely only to serve as an elusive ideal we might aim for.

Writing an informal style is easy—you just talk on paper. Writing a formal style is relatively easy, too, once you have the knack—you just haul out all the high-sounding and impersonal phrases you've seen other people use. But writing a good "General English" style is hard. It's hard because it requires a sophisticated control of *tone,* which is the most intangible but perhaps most consequential element in a writer's voice. As I said earlier, "General English" is essentially a happy compromise between formality and informality. This means it involves a mingling of contraries: formal and informal vocabulary, objectivity and subjectivity, impersonality and directness. All of these things affect tone. Part of the challenge, then—and it's a formidable one—is to get the right mix. That's as tricky as concocting a good sweet-and-sour sauce. The other part of the challenge is to work around the edges of these various extremes without taking a major tumble.

When, for example, will a colloquialism lend just the right note of easy informality, and when might it have the effect of cheapening a sentence? Or, to take the opposite problem, when will an unusual word add a nicely piquant effect, and when might it sound merely pretentious? Yet again: When will a personal touch be welcome, and when obtrusive? Guessing right requires a good ear, taste, and tact—all of them intuitive, finally, and acquired only through considerable reading and writing.

The question of style is obviously a large issue—at bottom, a moral issue—and one that we could go on and on with. We will, in fact, pursue it a little further in the next chapter. But to draw the matter to a temporary close, I'll simply tell you what I tell my students when the issue comes up in class and we're a minute away from the bell:

"Each time we write, we're making a choice as to the kind of person we prefer to be. Since it's so important, let's make that choice a conscious one for a change. Here's what it involves: 'Do I want to be authentically *me,* speaking my own thoughts in my own idiom, or am I content to be a pseudo-self, using borrowed thoughts, borrowed language, and a borrowed personality to gain the approval of a few literary traditionalists?'

"The assumptions we make about our reader are naturally going to condition that choice, since we never write in a vacuum. But instead of automatically assuming that he will reject authenticity, I recommend that you ask yourself: Is it likely that the average intelligent reader actually prefers to read the highly repressed, orthodox, formal style of discourse, or might he too not secretly regard it as all too often effete, stuffy, and boring?

"Sometimes, of course, stuffy or not, the formal style will seem to be the only one appropriate to the occasion, either because tradition decrees it or because the subject calls for an impersonal treatment. If you're writing a legal brief, for example, or a statement of corporate policy or a scientific paper, your job is to transmit technical information, not offer private reflections on it; and you'll show the reader that you understand that job by adopting a serious, judicial manner that discourages the leakage of subjective impressions.

"But, for heaven's sake, let's not allow ourselves to be slaves to blind convention—or unnecessary pomp, for that matter. Few situations are really so intrinsically formal as we're conditioned to believe. Just because everyone else is standing on ceremony in a given situation doesn't necessarily mean that it's obligatory, or that they *prefer* to; they may simply be afraid to be themselves, and may be just waiting for some free spirit to come along and give them the courage of their natural impulses. This holds as true for writing situations as it does for life in general. I suggest you keep in mind the example of Franklin Roosevelt. When he gave his periodic radio addresses to the American people, he could have adopted a lofty, presidential style. In fact, convention almost insisted on it. But Roosevelt blithely ignored convention, choosing instead to give what he called 'Fireside Chats'—personal, down-to-earth talks laced with colloquialisms and jokes. Here was a man who obviously listened to the promptings of his heart. He figured that the average citizen, like himself, would prefer relaxed plain talk to studied oratory. And he was proved right. Those talks helped make him one of the most endearing of modern presidents.

"Finally, I recommend that you be guided by what your own eyes and ears tell you, not merely by the so-called authorities. Just what *is* considered acceptable style today in serious writing? Look at the evidence—the magazines such as *Harper's, The Atlantic Monthly,* and *Newsweek*; the editorial columns of the *New York Times* and the *Los Angeles Times*; the latest books of nonfiction. You'll find that we're witnessing in this country a revolution in the notion of what constitutes a good style for serious writing—a movement toward greater naturalness, vigor, informality, and individuality. It was bound to happen. We see similar revolutions occurring in life styles, religious beliefs, sexual attitudes. When even the staid *New York Times* and *Wall Street Journal* permit contractions in their editorial columns, as they do now, you know that literary Victorianism is really on its way out." *

Now to move on to the tips. The two best ways I know of promoting an authentic and readable style are these:

> **1** Write with the assumption that your reader is a companionable friend with a warm sense of humor and an appreciation of simple straightforwardness.
>
> **2** Write as if you were actually talking to that friend, but talking with enough leisure to frame your thoughts concisely and interestingly.

If you tack these two tips on the wall in front of your writing desk and make a habit of continually glancing at them, I predict that the readability quotient of your prose style will take a dramatic leap upwards. Here are some additional tips:

3 Substitute the pronoun *that* for *which* wherever possible. The one is conversational, the other bookish. Reserve *which* for those places where a comma would normally precede it. Example: "The shortage, which has now reached critical proportions, is likely to remain a problem." Here the *which* clause merely adds some nonessential information and thus functions as a parenthesis. Contrast to: "The shortage that he spoke of is likely to remain a problem." Here the *that* clause serves to specify the particular shortage being referred

---

* Bergen Evans, co-author of *A Dictionary of American Usage* and one of the country's most respected experts on the subject, remarked as far back as 1962: "As written English is used by increasing millions and for more reasons than ever before, the language has become more utilitarian and more informal. Every publication in America today includes pages that would appear, to the purist of forty years ago, unbuttoned gibberish. Not that they are; they simply show that you can't hold the language of one generation up as a model for the next" ("But What's a Dictionary For?" *The Atlantic Monthly*, May 1962).

to; hence it defines or restricts the subject, "shortage," and mustn't be separated from it by commas. The rule is: if you can remove the clause without damaging the sense of the sentence, use *which* and a comma before it.

4 Use occasional contractions. They'll keep you from taking yourself too seriously, tell your reader that you're not a prude, and help you achieve a more natural, conversational rhythm in your style. The most popular contractions are those involving *am, are, is,* and *not.* Among that group the following are especially natural to the ear:

I'm
you're, we're, they're
he's, she's, here's
won't, wouldn't, don't, doesn't, can't

Contractions, though, are like kisses: when bestowed indiscriminately, they lose their effect, in fact seem cheap. Hold them in reserve. Save them for when you want to civilize an otherwise barbarous-sounding sentence like "Let us start now because I will not be in town tomorrow" or "Would you not think a stuffed shirt wrote this sentence?"

5 If you mean "I," *say* "I." Don't wrap your identity in such pomposities as "the writer" or "one" or "this author" or "we." Reserve "we" and "our" for those situations where you're referring to both your reader and yourself—i.e., where there really is more than one of you involved. Reserve "one" for when you mean "a person," as in "One would have to be a lawyer to understand that." When referring to the reader alone, address him as "you," not "the reader." The printed page already puts enough distance between the two of you. Why add to it?

6 Use dashes to isolate concluding phrases for emphasis or humorous effect. Pauline Kael is an artist with the dash. If you flip back and reread her reviews quoted in chapter 1, you'll get an idea of the kind of effects you can achieve with it yourself.

7 Use dialogue wherever your context warrants it—it's intrinsically dramatic. Also use imagined thoughts. Example:

Events inexorably force Enobarbus to a decision—an impossible one. It would seem that he's thinking here something like this: "My mind tells me to leave Antony for Rome. My heart tells me to leave Rome for Antony. Both courses of action are right, and both are wrong. To go either way is to deny a central fact of my existence. I am a Roman, but I am also a man. There seems to be only one solution: death. It will eliminate the need to choose."

8 As a general rule of thumb, if you have written three long sentences in a row, make your fourth a short one. And don't be afraid of the very short sentence. Sometimes even a single word works beautifully, as this example from humorist Gregg Hopkins shows:

> Many American parents have voiced the opinion that today's colleges are veritable breeding grounds for premarital sex. Nonsense. Each year, literally tens of students graduate with their virtue still intact.

9 The more abstract your argument, the more you should lace it with graphic illustrations, analogies, apt quotations, and concrete details. These are aids not only to your reader's understanding but also to his memory. In fact, he'll probably remember the illustration or analogy far longer than he will the abstract idea itself. If the illustration is a good one, though, he'll often be able to reconstruct the thought with a little effort, so it will have served its purpose twice over.

10 Keep your adjectives to a minimum. Let strong nouns do the work of adjectives. You'll find that this will simplify your style *and* give it more point. I think that Voltaire overstated the case a bit, though, when he observed, "The adjective is the enemy of the noun." A more sensible maxim is Twain's: "As to the Adjective: when in doubt, strike it out."

11 Avoid weak (trite) adverbs like *very, extremely, really,* and *terribly.* Instead of saying, "She was very upset by the news," say "She was shattered by the news." The use of *very* and its cognates usually betrays a distrust of the power of the word that follows it. If it's not as strong as you want it, find another word. There always is one.

12 Use the fewest words possible and the simplest words possible. Occasionally, to be sure, the longer word will be the only right word:

it may express the idea concisely, or contribute just the rhythm and texture wanted, or gratify your reader with the joy of surprise. (*Rectitude* and *chastening* in the Updike passage quoted in chapter 7 are examples.) But be warned: the more you surrender to the temptation to use big words—"gigundas," I call them—the further you are apt to stray from your true feelings and the more you will tend to write a style designed to impress rather than to serve the reader. Also, fancy prose can give a writer the delusion that he's really saying something significant, when it may be that he's using rhetoric defensively to conceal from himself how little he actually has to say. Oratory should never be asked to substitute for accuracy and truth. So, follow Henry Thoreau's famous advice, for your own protection: "Simplify, simplify." This may sound easy. It isn't. "To write simply is as difficult as to be good," sighed Somerset Maugham. Hemingway agreed: "Writing plain English is hard work."

13 Make sure that each sentence you write is manifestly connected to the ones immediately preceding and following it. There's no other way to achieve smooth continuity.

14 In a long essay or report, periodically summarize your argument so that your reader will be able to keep his bearings. It's often effective to cast these summaries in the form of brief transitional paragraphs, perhaps only three or four sentences in length. They make a welcome change of pace and serve to graphically separate the stages in your argument.

15 If you enjoy putting questions to your reader, it's prudent to pose them at the beginning of a paper and answer them. If you put them at the tail end and leave your reader the job of answering them, you may achieve only confusion, not resolution.

16 Use semicolons to reduce choppiness, particularly when you have several related sentences in parallel structure. Also use them for a change of pace. (See the section on semicolons in chapter 12 for illustrations.)

17 Read your prose aloud. *Always* read your prose aloud. If it sounds as if it's come out of a machine or a social scientist's report (which is approximately the same thing), spare your reader and rewrite it.

18 Instead of always saying "first" and "second," occasionally use the numerals themselves in parentheses. It's a superstition that numerals have no place in serious writing. For proof of this, browse through any major anthology of expository prose—*The Norton Reader,* for example.

19 Written-out numbers such as *twenty-eight* are unwieldy. Most authorities recommend that you use the numerals themselves over 20 and the written form for all numbers under 20. But why write *eighteen* when it's so much simpler to write *18?* What can possibly be objectionable about *18?* The purist would probably answer: "It lacks the dignity of *eighteen*." Such a person doubtless undresses with the lights out. I recommend that you use the numerals themselves from 10 on and congratulate yourself on your common sense.

20 If you begin a sentence with *and* or *but* (and you should occasionally), don't put a comma after it. You want to speed up your prose with those words, and the comma would simply cancel out any gain. The comma is necessary only if a parenthetical clause immediately follows that first word—e.g., "But, from all the evidence, that proves to be a sound conclusion."

21 Give free rein to your sense of humor wherever possible. What's called "serious writing" need not be solemn writing. F. L. Lucas, in his excellent book *Style,* observed with characteristic good sense: "No manual of style that I know has a word to say of good humour; and yet, for me, a lack of it can sometimes blemish all the literary beauties and blandishments ever taught."

22 There's as much psychology in paragraphing properly as in any other aspect of writing. Long paragraphs send off alarms in most readers' minds; very short paragraphs suggest insubstantiality and flightiness; a long succession of medium-length paragraphs indicates no imagination and proves monotonous. Moral: vary your pacing to keep your piece alive and vital, as Dr. Seuss advised.

23 Choose your title with care. Make it accurately descriptive (leave the "teasing" title to cute writers) and try to give it zing. Remember, it's your reader's introduction to your paper. A pedestrian title is about as welcoming as a burned-out motel sign.

24 Avoid exclamation points, which have been cheapened by comic-strip cartoonists (who haven't yet discovered the period) and by advertising copywriters. For more on this, see the section on exclamation points in chapter 12.

25 If you've written a paragraph that sounds heavy and tortured, put down your pencil and ask yourself: "If I were actually speaking these thoughts to a friend, how would I probably say them?" Then go ahead and talk them *out loud,* and when you're finished, write down as nearly as you can recall what you said. The chances are good that many of your talked-out sentences will be an improvement over the earlier, labored version of them.

26 Another tip for the same crisis is this: Take a 10-minute break and read a few paragraphs of a writer whose style you relish. Try to *soak in* that style; try to feel yourself actually writing those paragraphs as you read them. Then say to yourself, "OK, now, how would Blank rewrite my paragraph?" and let yourself go. This usually works. And even when it doesn't, it will at least enable you to gain a fresh perspective on what you've written. That's half the battle right there.

9 *Superstitions*

Above all, we believe that naturalness is unnatural, that informality is unacceptable, and that individuality is unpardonable.

TOTELARIAN CREED

To be nobody-but-yourself—in a world which is doing its best, night and day, to make you everybody else—means to fight the hardest battle which any human being can fight; and never stop fighting.

e. e. cummings

This chapter concerns literary prudes. More specifically, it concerns the near-religion they make of Formal English, the superstitions they would have us accept, and the serious moral implications of their whole ideology.

I confess I'm of several minds about how to treat this race of people. Part of me wants to be gentle. I was once a literary prude myself—in fact, I still bear some of the marks—and I know that they mean well. Another part of me wants to poke fun at their ludicrous rigidity and solemnity. Who cannot smile at someone prepared to go to war over a split infinitive? Yet a third part of me, more aware every day of the insidious thought control (through language control) implicit in their dogma, aware, too, that their influence far exceeds their numbers, and noting that 1984 is drawing ever closer, wants to explode in the terms of an outraged moralist, yes, even dress for battle myself in defense of that split infinitive. I have no idea how these three impulses can happily mesh. Perhaps the thing to do is let them fight it out among themselves. Well, without further mulling, here goes.

Literary prudes, Donald Lloyd once observed, are the people who put triumphant exclamation marks in the margins of library books.

They make themselves more readily identifiable, though, through their talk. Just to be sure we're thinking of the same race of people, I'll provide some samples of it: "But of course one must *never* split infinitives"; "Well, the Rule says, you know, that contractions are unacceptable in serious prose"; "William, when are you going to learn that 'I' *must* be followed by 'shall,' not 'will'?"; "Never say 'It's me,' dear. Say 'It is I.' "

These people arrived at their literary prudishness through a variety of routes: some through a puristic concern for the language which gradually rigidified into morbid scrupulosity; some through ignorance reinforced by others' ignorance; some through a hunger for the security of dogma and absolutes; and some, it would seem, merely through the appeals of snobbery and elitism. Upon arrival at their mental state, they were at once ushered into a large congregation of true-believers whose faith is embalmed Formal English. Unaccountably, until now their faith has gone nameless. I will repair that oversight and christen it "The One True English Language Sect" (or "TOTELS" for short).

The history of this sect, its periodic Holy Causes such as the war against *Webster III,** its august leadership, its diverse membership —all make for a fascinating story, but too long a one for this little book. I will merely focus on TOTELS' Articles of Faith, Creed, and Rules, for these are more directly pertinent to the layman, and I can dispose of them quickly.

First, the Articles of Faith. These provide TOTELS with its ideological foundation, such as it is. But they also perform an invaluable function once they are accepted: they allow the believer to look at all contrary evidence with a tranquil heart. Indeed, as if by a miracle, they often permit the believer not even to *see* any contrary evidence. The chief Articles, which I have taken the liberty to translate into plain English, are these:

Article I: The English Language is a system of Laws, not—as the new Linguistic Heresy claims—merely a system of human conventions.

Article II: Being a system of Laws, the Language was meant to be

---

* This is an abbreviated title for *Webster's Third New International Dictionary.* For a full chronicle of this bloody war, see the *Harbrace Guide to Dictionaries,* ed. Kenneth Wilson et al. (New York: Harcourt, Brace, 1963).

static, not dynamic. Hence any changes in the Language are abnormal and are to be regarded as Corruptions.

Article III: Because of Articles I and II, Correct Usage depends upon adherence to the Rules which our Elders have sagely inferred from the Laws of the Language.

Following these Articles, and springing out of them, as it were, are the TOTELarian Creed and Rules. The Creed, which the devoutest members know without ever having to read it, runs thus:

We believe in Rules, Authority, and the One True English Language.

We believe in the sanctity of Formal English, which shall ever be revered for its elaborate syntax, baroque sentences, ornate words, and stiff expressions, all of which we pledge ourselves laboriously to employ.

Above all, we believe that naturalness is unnatural, that informality is unacceptable, and that individuality is unpardonable. Amen.

The Rules, unfortunately, cannot be reprinted so easily, for they are scattered among many Sacred Texts (vulgarly known as old grammar books) and run into the thousands. The seven Core Rules must suffice here. Everyone, I trust, remembers them, since they have been circulated far outside the faith and chanted with some regularity. They are, of course, the Seven Nevers:

1 Never begin a sentence with *and* or *but.*
2 Never use contractions.
3 Never refer to the reader as *you.*
4 Never use the first-person pronoun, *I.*
5 Never end a sentence with a preposition.
6 Never split an infinitive.
7 Never write a paragraph containing only a single sentence.

There you have it in sketchy outline—the TOTELarian ideology, its Articles of Faith, its Creed, and its Seven Nevers. Now, for the remainder of the chapter, I would like to wrestle with the Nevers in the manner of an exorcist with unholy demons, earnestly hoping that I may free you from their hold forever. If you can stand the sight of them again, read on.

1. "Never begin a sentence with 'and' or 'but'"

The many English teachers who still teach this superstition do so, apparently, for one or more of the following reasons: (a) they were taught it themselves at an impressionable age and have never since thought to question its legitimacy; (b) they hope to discourage anything smacking of informality in student writing, perhaps in part because what informality they have seen in student prose has tended to read like banal cafeteria chatter; (c) they can use this rule as an expedient way of forcing students to move beyond simple sentences ("The government's new program is long overdue") to compound ones ("The government's new program is long overdue, but implementing it will be difficult").

The fact remains, though, that *and* and *but* are perfectly valid ways of beginning a sentence. You see it done all the time by professional writers, and often to great effect. Take, for example, Bergen Evans. In his *Atlantic Monthly* article cited in the last chapter, a stirring defense of the then newly published *Webster III,* Mr. Evans begins 29 sentences with *but* and, coincidentally, another 29 with *and.* By doing so, he manages to speed up the pace of his prose, smooth it out, and increase its conversational tone to the point where one has the impression of actually hearing the man speak. It's uncanny; it's also a model example of the "General English" style. I'll quote two short paragraphs so you can see for yourself:

> The ultimate of "permissiveness," singled out by almost every critic for special scorn, was the inclusion in the Third International of *finalize.* It was this, more than any other one thing, that was given as the reason for sticking to the good old Second International—that "peerless authority on American English," as the *Times* called it. But if it was such an authority, why didn't they look into it? They would have found *finalize* if they had.
>
> And why shouldn't it be there? It exists. It's been recorded for two generations. Millions employ it every day. Two Presidents of the United States—men of widely differing cultural backgrounds—have used it in formal statements. And so has the Secretary-General of the United Nations, a man of most unusual linguistic attainments. It isn't permitting the word but omitting it that would break faith with the reader.

I should caution you, though, to use the *and* or *but* sentence with restraint. Just because it's legitimate doesn't mean that it can't grow tiresome. Mr. Evans' 29 *and*s and 29 *but*s manage to avoid monotony only by being sprinkled through ten densely packed pages— and, I might add, by being used only where the occasion genuinely warrants them.

2. "Never use contractions"

If you believe, with the TOTELarians, that "naturalness is unnatural, and informality is unacceptable," then no amount of reasoning will persuade you that contractions have a place in serious writing. You will even be able to close your eyes to all those instances where respected writers *do* use them in serious writing. (The two paragraphs just quoted from Bergen Evans' article contained four such instances, by the way. Observe, too, the passages quoted earlier from Updike, White, Kael, Fitzgerald, and Michener.)

We could go around and around with the question of contractions. But in the final analysis it really comes down to nothing more than how our taste and values incline—that plus what we imagine our reader will find acceptable. Perhaps this last point is the heart of it, even for the TOTELarians, for what writer—and particularly what fastidious writer—doesn't want to make peace with his reader? As I pointed out earlier, the fear of rejection is potent; each of us, I suspect, can identify with T. S. Eliot's Prufrock or John Lennon's Eleanor Rigby. If we imagine our reader to be rigid and frowning, as our classroom experiences have conditioned most of us to, and if we thus imagine he will approve of us only in our starched-collar manner, we will usually wear that manner, however much we secretly abhor it. It's the same in writing as in life. Each is always imitating the other.

I think, though, that we might try paying the reader a compliment: writing as if he preferred reading unaffected, unsolemn, conversational prose to the boring and pretentious Formal variety. I think, too, that we might take a second look at the popular assumption that one can't—or shouldn't—be informal and serious at the same time. Objectively considered, what is more agreeable than such a mixture? Robert Frost observed:

> The style is the man. Rather say the style is the way the man takes himself; and to be at all charming or even bearable, the way is almost rigidly prescribed. If it is with outer seriousness, it must be with inner humor. If it is with outer humor, it must be with inner seriousness. Neither one alone without the other under it will do.

To my mind, a writer who never uses contractions is akin to someone whose outer seriousness has no inner humor under it. But the other side of the coin is equally true: a writer who constantly uses contractions is analogous to someone whose outer humor has no inner seriousness under it.

I would only repeat the admonition I offered in the last chapter: contractions are best used in moderation. When your ear tells you that the rhythm of a particular sentence seems to require a contraction, go ahead and use it without apology. It's perfectly acceptable in a "General English" style. (In fact, it's hard to write in such a style *without* using occasional contractions.) But where a contraction is not required, it's best not to use one, for to do so is to risk overweighting your style on the side of colloquialness.

3. "Never refer to the reader as 'you' "

The alternatives, of course, are never to refer to him at all or else to refer to him as "the reader." The first alternative is frequently difficult and nearly always bad psychology, for it contributes to what critic Wayne Booth has termed the "pedant's stance." As he defines it, that stance

> consists of ignoring or underplaying the personal relationship of speaker and audience and depending entirely on statements about a subject—that is, the notion of a job to be done for a particular audience is left out. . . . The writer who assumes that it is enough merely to write an exposition of what he happens to know on the subject will produce the kind of essay that soils our scholarly journals, written not for readers but for bibliographies.

The second alternative is equally bad psychology because it is so utterly depersonalizing and stuffy. What reader wants to be addressed as "the reader"? It's akin to saying, in conversation, "I'm glad to hear the listener has recovered from his cold."

You can see that it's the old issue in another guise: Is naturalness unnatural, and is informality unacceptable? The first part of that question I trust answers itself; the second part of it is answered by daily experience. As Theodore Bernstein observes in his recent book on outmoded rules of English usage, *Miss Thistlebottom's Hobgoblins*: "Informality in all kinds of writing has been in the ascendancy in recent times and now the indefinite *you* is accepted and widely used." Mr. Bernstein ought to know. He is not only former assistant managing editor of the *New York Times* but also served in Paris as founding editor of the *Times'* International Edition.

I only want to add to his remark the caution that while *you* is widely used, it can be overused. Just as some speakers wear out our ears with "you know" punctuating every sentence, so some writers push a close relationship upon us with the constantly reiterated *you*. We instinctively pull back from such chumminess, regarding it as an unwanted bear-hug. Moral: If you don't need to say *you*, don't. If you do need to, say it without embarrassment exactly as you would in conversation.

4. "Never use the first-person pronoun, 'I' "

The alternatives recall those just described under Rule #3: either you practice complete self-effacement, in which case you disappear altogether from your prose, or else you attempt the closest thing to it, self-transcendence, in which case you elect to become either an objectification of yourself (*the writer*) or something more than yourself (the royal *we*). This rule, and the alternatives it allows, clearly assumes that the best expository prose is the most scrupulously impersonal. In theory, then, the best prose would come from a machine, which is precisely what many TOTELarians attempt to imitate. (I refer you once again to their Creed: ". . . and individuality is unpardonable.") Little wonder that their prose is invariably bloodless and boring: all the life has been drained out of it.

But this is just the beginning of the rule's ludicrousness. Since what we write is presumably what we believe and feel, it is logically inconsistent to put up the pretense that it is scientifically detached and Pure Thought, and that our words just dropped out of thin air onto paper. Moreover, the pretense itself is a piece of absurdity. It's akin to ducking behind a screen every time you say something in conversation so as to persuade your listener that he is hearing merely some Voice, some disembodied Intelligence, speaking to him.

Common sense and honesty recommend simple forthrightness, I think: we should feel free to acknowledge our convictions as *our* convictions. We need not be loud about it, of course—we don't wish to appear egocentric or hopelessly subjective in our viewpoints. And we needn't label every view as our own, for who else's will they be thought to be? But let us allow some of our personality, which means some of our *I*, to come through our style. Let us, in short, be ourselves.

5. "Never end a sentence with a preposition"

H. W. Fowler, the preeminent British authority on questions of usage, wrote a crushing rebuttal to this piece of nonsense in his *Dictionary of Modern English Usage,* a book you should buy. I will quote only his conclusions and leave you to read on your own the wealth of evidence he marshaled to support them:

> It is a cherished superstition that prepositions must, in spite of the incurable English instinct for putting them late . . . be kept true to their name [*preposition* derives from a Latin word meaning "to place in front"] and placed before the word they govern. . . . Those who lay down the universal principle that final prepositions are "inelegant" are unconsciously trying to deprive the English language of a valuable idiomatic resource, which has been used freely by all our greatest writers except those whose instinct for English idiom has been overpowered by notions of correctness derived from Latin standards. The legitimacy of the prepositional ending in literary English must be uncompromisingly maintained; in respect of elegance or inelegance, every example must be judged not by any arbitrary rules, but on its own merits. . . .

Perhaps it was Winston Churchill, though, even more than Fowler, who delivered the *coup de grâce* to this superstition. When the old statesman had his attention called to a final preposition lurking in his prose, he exploded with: "This is the type of arrant pedantry, up with which I shall not put."

6. "Never split an infinitive"

I am reminded of a cartoon in *The New Yorker*. Satan is seated on his throne in Hell, silently glowering. Before him stands one of his lieutenants, obviously worried, asking uncertainly: "If everybody's doing it, is it still a sin?"

Splitting an infinitive (for example, saying "to fully cooperate" rather than "fully to cooperate") wasn't always deemed a sin, and it's not a recent phenomenon either. In fact, infinitives have been split repeatedly by reputable authors (Shakespeare among them) ever since the 14th century. But in the 18th and 19th centuries, a group of TOTELarian grammarians set about trying to "regularize" English grammar—that is, make it conform to laws—and among other things, they decreed that infinitives should not be split by adverbs. The principle they invoked was that related words belong together. Since the infinitive form of a verb requires the preposition *to* plus the verb, these are logically related words—a unit of syntax, in other words.

All this, at first blush, seems rational enough. Unfortunately, not just grammarians use the language. People use it too, and people will do what they will do; and one thing most people instinctively will do is split infinitives. We have just heard Fowler speak of "the incurable English instinct" for putting prepositions at the end of sentences; here we have yet another instance of human intractability—or is it untutored wisdom again?

So much for background. Now, the questions we must answer are: (a) Do the infinitive-splitters (i.e., virtually the entire English-speaking population) have the *right* to do what they're doing, and (b) Do they have defensible *reasons* for doing what they're doing?

First question *a.* If the language were a system of natural laws, and if our grammarians were gifted with infallible minds with which to divine the workings of those laws, then we would have to accept the TOTELarian view that infinitive-splitters have no right to take the liberties they do. But those aren't the facts. The facts are that the language is nothing more than a system of human conventions, and that it's constantly changing. (If you doubt this, try reading Chaucer's English without a trot.) As a result, usage is relative. Furthermore, the grammarians are as fallible as any other mechanics. They've proved it by ignoring (until recently) the dynamic nature of the language. So it comes down to a case of *The People* vs. *The Grammarians*. The verdict: The majority must rule because they *will* rule. Besides, it's their language.

The infinitive-splitters have the right, then. But this still leaves unanswered the question of whether their practice is sensible. Should we, in short, go out and imitate them?

So, on to question *b*: Do the infinitive-splitters have defensible reasons? Most of them probably never think about it; they just do it. But if they tried to rationalize their practice, they would more than likely advance three justifications. First, the split infinitive usually sounds better—that is, it has a more idiomatic rhythm to it, in part at least because we invariably hear infinitives split in common speech. Second, it allows the modifying adverb to be positioned where it will receive the most notice, which is directly ahead of the verb. (Example: "To really know her, you have to live with her.") Third, since grammarians recommend that modifiers should come, if possible, next to the word they modify, the adverb has as much right to sit next to the verb as the preposition *to*—and perhaps more right, not only because it is the more weighty of the two words but because it frequently changes the very sense of the verb. All three of these reasons strike me as commonsensical. There certainly must be something to them, for why else would so many people instinctively use the split construction?

As for my own practice, like most writers I go by ear and sense. When my ear tells me that a split construction sounds more natural, and when my sense assures me there's no ambiguity, I happily split the infinitive. If my ear tells me it's a toss-up, I don't split it because there's no pressing reason to. In general, though, I concur with the eminent grammarian George Curme, who argued in his book *Syntax*: "The split infinitive is an improvement of English expression." Any skeptic who takes the trouble to read Curme's massively documented, nine-page scholarly analysis of the issue will find it hard to argue with that conclusion.

7. "Never write a paragraph containing only a single sentence"

Generally this rule is sound. What makes it so offensive is the dogmatic "Never." Mr. Bernstein rightly says in *Miss Thistlebottom's Hobgoblins*: "One cannot be arbitrary about paragraphing. It is a means of grouping thoughts, but much more it is a visual device. Much depends on the subject, the typography, the purpose of what is being written, the readers to whom it is addressed and the conditions under which they are likely to read it."

Take newspaper stories, for instance. The one-sentence paragraph is ideally suited to them. It simplifies the reporter's task of presenting his facts in a descending level of importance; it enables the hurried reader to digest those facts quickly; it offsets the tediousness created by narrow columns and small type; and so on.

Unfortunately, though, because we encounter the one-sentence paragraph most frequently in news stories, most of us are inclined to believe that it is a device best left to journalists. It's legitimate for them, we grant, but it isn't quite respectable in so-called "serious" writing.

This view is both prudish and misguided. Any number of reputable works prove it. One I read recently is Robert Selph Henry's *The Story of the Confederacy,* considered by many historians to be among the indispensable studies of the American Civil War—a work, I might add, surely as distinguished for its elegant, vivid prose style as for its scholarly brilliance. Mr. Henry, I note, uses 17 one-sentence paragraphs in the first two chapters alone. Indeed, he opens the book with two in quick succession:

> The Confederacy was a belated attempt to exercise the right of a state to withdraw from the United States of America.
> Because it was belated, because it opposed a mere right in the abstract to the concrete force of economics and the inevitable trend of history, because it was burdened with the defense of the anachronism of slavery, it failed.

Basically, there are three situations in essay-writing that can occasion a one-sentence paragraph: (a) when you wish to emphasize a crucial point that might otherwise be buried; (b) when you wish to dramatize a transition from one stage in your argument to the next; and (c) when instinct tells you that your reader is tiring and would appreciate a mental rest-station.

The one-sentence paragraph is a valuable device. You can italicize with it, vary your pace with it, lighten your prose texture with it, signpost your argument with it. But it's also a potentially dangerous device. Be sure you don't overdo your dramatics. Also, be sure your sentence is strong enough to stand up under the extra attention it is bound to receive when set off by itself. Houseplants wilt in direct sun; so, in a manner of speaking, do many sentences.

10 *The art of revising*

Interviewer: How much rewriting do you do?

Hemingway: It depends. I rewrote the ending of *Farewell to Arms,* the last page of it, thirty-nine times before I was satisfied.

Interviewer: Was there some technical problem there? What was it that had stumped you?

Hemingway: Getting the words right.

Paris Review INTERVIEW

11 *Proofreading*

Don't expect your reader to accept a piece of writing that you wouldn't accept yourself.

Proofreading is like the quality-control stage at the end of an assembly line. Think of it in these terms and you'll see why you shouldn't consider a paper finished until you have proofread it with finicky thoroughness. Proofreading is your responsibility, not the reader's. But even beyond the question of responsibility is the crucial matter of basic reader psychology. Your object is to court your reader, not alienate him. If you give him a carelessly proofread paper, you hazard his concluding at least one of these opinions about you: (a) you are an undisciplined, lazy individual; (b) you will probably be found to be as grubbyminded a thinker as you are a proofreader; and (c) you are the kind of writer whom it's going to be pure drudgery to read. It may be unjust, I agree, but it's reality.

Proofreading involves two things: spotting your errors and then correcting them in a way that is instantly intelligible to your reader. Correcting them intelligibly, though, requires that you be familiar with the conventional proofreaders' marks. This takes but a few minutes' study. A complete list of the symbols can be found at the back of most good dictionaries. (*The American Heritage Dictionary* prints its list, though, alongside the entry for *proofread*. This list, incidentally, provides the clearest explanation of proofreaders' marks I have seen.) Some dictionaries, such as *Webster's New Collegiate,* even supply a sample of an error-ridden text that has been properly corrected so that you can see how the various marks are applied.

Below are suggestions on how to correct some of the most common errors:

1 If you have left out a word or phrase, put a caret (∧) just below the line at the place where the omission occurred and then write in the word or phrase directly above the caret. Example:

word or
Write in the∧phrase.

2 If you have omitted an entire sentence, put a caret where the omission occurred, write "See over for insert" in the adjacent margin, and write the sentence on the back of the page. If the omission exceeds one or two sentences, it may be best to retype the whole page.

3 If you have used the wrong word or badly misspelled a word, draw a line through it and write the correction directly *above* it. However, if the misspelling involves the mistyping or omission of merely a single letter, put a caret just below the line at the place where the error occurred, cross out the error, and then write in the letter directly above it.

4 If you wish to delete a period or comma, simply circle it. (Note: this procedure will suffice except when submitting a manuscript for typesetting—i.e., publication. At such a time, you can delete a period or comma only by running the delete sign (℘) through the mark, since a circle around a comma changes it to a period.)

5 If your typewriter has skipped a space in the typing of a word, close up that space with a *pair* of horizontal parentheses, not just one. Example:

Close up that sp⌒ace.

6 If letters or words need transposing, proceed thus:

Jack ⌐Jill⌐and⌐went up t⌐h⌐/hill.

7 If you wish to designate a sentence as the beginning of a new paragraph, put the paragraph sign (¶) just before it and well above the line where it will be clearly visible.

It frequently happens that, during either the writing or the proofreading of a paper, you are uncertain as to the correctness of an idiom, a punctuation mark, an assertion, or whatever. At such times, I recommend that you put a circled number in the adjacent margin and then, at the end of your essay, write a corresponding number followed by a note explaining your confusion. Example:

①   Is "alternative" correct here, or should I have said "alternate" instead?

You will want to leave a space, of course, below each question for your teacher to write in his answer. Students who have used this procedure report that it is very helpful to them. Among other advantages, it gives them courage to try out the new and the strange. Its chief advantage, though, is that it gives them quick feedback on questions which they might not otherwise receive answers to.

Odds & ends

What follows is a little grab-bag of notes on various stylistic and procedural matters—punctuation, conventions, usage, and the like. This section makes no attempt to anticipate all of your possible questions on these subjects; by the same token it doesn't waste your time telling you what in all likelihood you already know. It merely tries to clear up some basic, recurring questions that have plagued the majority of students I have known, be they freshmen or seniors.

Since we all balk at accepting—let alone remembering—rules handed down to us as arbitrary fiats, I've tried wherever possible to explain the Why behind the conventions and procedures I discuss here. I've also tried to anticipate some problems by noting the various traps which students fall into as a result of misunderstanding these conventions. And finally, I've tried to turn a normally boring subject, punctuation, into an interesting one by focusing on the resources of the various marks rather than on the tedious rules governing them. My hope is that the examples I provide will themselves teach the rules and prove entertaining in the bargain.

I scant grammar here, partly because it lies outside the strict province of this book and partly because it's already been well treated elsewhere—I'm thinking primarily of the *Prentice-Hall Handbook for Writers* and the *Harbrace College Handbook*. These are two of the most popular college texts, and deservedly so.

For further help on questions of usage, I recommend Theodore

Bernstein's *The Careful Writer,* Bergen and Cornelia Evans' *A Dictionary of Contemporary American Usage,* H. W. Fowler's *A Dictionary of Modern English Usage,* and Porter Perrin's *Writer's Guide and Index to English.* All of them are not only encyclopedic but genuinely readable, and at least one of them belongs on your reference shelf. It will quickly prove indispensable.

12 *Punctuation*

Punctuation, to most people, is a set of arbitrary and rather silly rules you find in printers' style books and in the back pages of school grammars. Few people realize that it is the most important single device for making things easier to read.

RUDOLF FLESCH

Semicolons

The average college freshman isn't ready for semicolons. He hasn't yet discovered any need for them, nor is he particularly eager to. To him, they look forbiddingly exotic—about as tempting as a plate of snails. The literary gourmets can have them; he'll stick with his familiar comma and period—though if the truth be known, he isn't entirely comfortable even with these. Confessed one sophomore, a veteran of the trenches: "The first semester of Freshman English I used to write only short sentences so I wouldn't have to put commas in."

Practice and experience usually bring a change of attitude, though —especially if that experience includes extensive reading. Eventually a writer will feel himself ready to handle longer, more complex sentences; he will be concerned with tightening up his slack phrasing; he will have developed a delight in balancing off ideas against one another; he will be actively looking about for ways of adding variety to his style; and with his new confidence he will have developed an interest in doing things with the language beyond what the more routine punctuation marks allow. This is when he will suddenly begin discovering the manifold resources of the semicolon. He'll see that it can serve him well in each of these areas.

Before I explain how, I should explain the way the semicolon works. Basically, it functions like the automatic coupling device on railroad cars: it allows you to join two or three or even more related sentences so as to form a single, complex thought—something we do in conversation all the time with half-pauses. It's a sign that says to the reader, "Take a brief rest here to gather in the preceding clause, but then keep right on going because this thought isn't finished yet."

Because the sentences you're joining are manifestly related, you don't need to insert *and* or *but* or any other connective between them (although you may if you wish to); all you need is the semicolon. It's that simple. And you'll never have any trouble with it if you remember one caveat: don't try to join anything less than *complete sentences* with it. There's an easy test: *If you can replace your semicolon with a period, your construction is OK, but if you can't, substitute a comma for it.* The only time you can ignore this rule is when you're using the semicolon as a kind of super comma to cleanly separate lengthy items listed in series. (More on that later.)

Let's look at some examples. Suppose you had these two sentences:

A beauty is a woman you notice. A charmer is one who notices you.

Now these sentences would profit from linking, especially if they were surrounded by many short ones like them. Kept separate, they read choppily; and what they're expressing is really a single thought —i.e., the difference between a beauty and a charmer. One way to link them—the most popular way—is with a comma followed by a coordinating conjunction such as *and* or *but*. Thus:

A beauty is a woman you notice, while a charmer is one who notices you.

The alternative way to link them is with a semicolon:

A beauty is a woman you notice; a charmer is one who notices you.
—ADLAI STEVENSON

Note how much crisper, leaner, and more emphatic this last version is than either of the earlier ones. The first version is weak because it spreads out the witty contrast over two sentences. The second version is weak because it's doing all the reader's thinking for him: the *while* feels too explicit, plus it's one word too many—a glaring fault in clauses that are otherwise so spare. The final version rectifies all these problems. It's unified, uncluttered, perfectly balanced, and dramatic. This is what it means to do things with the language beyond what the more routine punctuation marks allow.

As you become more familiar with the semicolon, you'll discover that it offers several benefits.

First is variety. "All pleasure consists in variety," observed Dr. Johnson two centuries ago, and this is certainly true for readers. The comma-plus-conjunction formula, the most popular way of joining sentences, grows tiresome after a while—as tiresome as a succession of simple sentences ending in periods. An occasional change in the formula not only gives the reader something different to look at (variety for the eye) but also changes the rhythm and pace of your sentences (variety for the mind's ear).

Second is greater compression. The semicolon is efficient: it allows you to eliminate most of those conjunctions or prepositions that are obligatory with the comma—words like *whereas, because, for, or, but, while, and*. Each time you condense a thought, you automatically increase its power of effect. You're doing something analogous to distilling whiskey: you're extracting the concentrate, the pure essence of the thought. In the example below, try mentally replacing the semicolon with a comma plus the word *for*. You'll find, I think, that the sentence reads exactly one word too long that way:

Many American lawyers would disagree; they have long prided themselves as generalists, able to perform any legal task.—*Newsweek*

Third is tightened contrasts. As our first example by Adlai Stevenson illustrated, the semicolon is ideally suited for linking contrasting ideas that are parallel in structure. At such times it acts like the fulcrum of a seesaw, balancing the ideas off against one another. The effect is that of a couplet—neat, concise, epigrammatic.

Fourth is unity. The semicolon permits a smooth, quick, coherent grouping of ideas into one tidy bundle. An example will make this graphically evident. In the paragraph below, Mark Twain cites four reasons for his once being ignorant that there was anything wrong with slavery. Had he not linked them, the effect would have been noticeably choppy; and had he tried linking them with commas and conjunctions, the effect would have been chaotic. But using semicolons and roughly parallel structure, he is able to pull them all neatly together into one coherent sentence:

> In my school-boy days I had no aversion to slavery. I was not aware that there was anything wrong about it. No one arraigned it in my hearing; the local papers said nothing against it; the local pulpit taught us that God approved it, that it was a holy thing, and that the doubter need only look in the Bible if he wished to settle his mind— and then the texts were read aloud to us to make the matter sure; if the slaves had an aversion, they were wise and said nothing. In Hannibal we seldom saw a slave misused; on the farm, never.

Incidentally, while that last semicolon looks like a violation of the rule about never joining anything less than complete sentences, it's really not. The words *on the farm, never* are an elliptical construction with the comma correctly used to mark the omission. What the reader does is mentally translate those words to mean "on the farm we never saw a slave misused"—a syntactically complete clause.

Now that you know the benefits of semicolons, you may be interested in studying the occasions where they prove particularly useful. Below is a list of four such occasions (some of them overlapping). There are others, to be sure, but these I think are the principal ones:

1 When you have two or more sentences which you wish the reader to understand as parts of a single thought:

> Training is everything. The peach was once a bitter almond; cauliflower is nothing but cabbage with a college education.
>
> —MARK TWAIN

2 When a sentence is so long, or so complex, that the reader would welcome a mental rest station along the way:

Psychoanalysis assumes that creative writers do their work out of profound inner dictates and in response to the ways in which their emotions and their views of the world have been formed. With all the world to choose from, they invariably select subjects closest to their inner feelings; and when they choose subjects seemingly alien to them, they invariably alter them to correspond to their personal condition, even though what emerges may seem, to the uninitiated, remote and unrelated.—LEON EDEL

3 When two or more related sentences are parallel in structure and thus invite pairing to set off either their contrast or likeness:

Some [football critics] would create a sliding scale making long kicks worth more points than short ones; others would return the ball to the line of scrimmage instead of the defenders' 20-yard line after missed kicks, making it riskier to attempt long ones.—PETE AXTHELM

As in all off-year elections, many of this year's scattered races were decided on purely local issues. In Detroit, for example, the voters cast their ballots along racial lines to elect the city's first back mayor; in New York, the local Democratic organization overwhelmed three lackluster rivals to pull off Controller Abraham Beame's mayoral victory.—*The New York Times*

4 When you wish to separate cleanly the various items in a series, particularly when commas occur within one or more members of the series; also when you wish to separate the items into classes, as in the first of the following examples:

Among its 35 or so working members are Ivan Allen Jr., the former mayor of Atlanta, and William Baker, the president of Bell Labs; Mary Wells Lawrence, of her own advertising agency, and Clare Boothe Luce; Daniel Patrick Moynihan, now ambassador to India, and Sol Linowitz, former ambassador to the Organization of American States.—*Newsweek*

Of course, essential to any good history or memoir is the venerable triad of rules: to respect the facts enough to keep burrowing for them, especially when they confound your preconceptions; to care enough

about your subject to express judgments clearly, vigorously and if
necessary, in a way that may antagonize; and withal, to exercise
restraint on yourself so that what you call history or memoir is not
an emanation of your own prejudices and self-interests but a work
which makes an honest and sustained effort to deserve that fine old
adjective, fair.—ERIC F. GOLDMAN

The recordings, she said, were full of "funny things"—the President
plunking his feet on the desk, where the bug was, with an impact
"like a bomb"; fragments of talk drowned out by rattling china, by a
marching band blaring outside, by Mr. Nixon inexplicably whistling
during meetings; hopeless scrambles when four people talked at once
"and you couldn't get one voice."—*Newsweek*

I've perhaps glutted you with information about the semicolon,
but I'd like to make one last point. From time to time you'll hear it
said that semicolons make the tone of one's writing heavier, more
formal. This is twaddle. The misconception arises because semicolons tend to congregate in academic writing, which is often co-
lossally ponderous—ponderous *not* because of the semicolons but
because of plain bad writing: pretentious, jargonistic diction; overlong sentences and paragraphs; humorlessness; a dearth of metaphors
and analogies; and so on. The charge, then, amounts to guilt by
association.

If you need proof that semicolons can mix agreeably with a readable style, go to the nonfiction of Mark Twain, one of America's
most consistently readable stylists. You'll find approximately half a
dozen semicolons per page. Or go to the writings of George Bernard
Shaw, one of England's wittiest stylists. You'll find the same thing.
Better still—since it's closer at hand—open any copy of *Newsweek*.
As my examples show, the pages of that magazine are sprinkled with
semicolons, yet I've never heard *Newsweek* called heavy or formal.

It all comes down to who's using them, and how, and how often.
Like anything else, semicolons can be used to excess. They can begin
calling attention to themselves, can begin looking gimmicky, can even
overcompress a writer's ideas on occasion. But when they're used
moderately—only at the most opportune times—and when a writer
is taking pains to write for his reader rather than to impress him,
semicolons can seem like the grammarians' happiest invention.

Commas

Most students have trouble with commas. Where do you put them in? When can you leave them out? If you demand a definitive answer, lock yourself in a padded cell with one of the thick handbooks on grammar. If you'll settle for something incomplete but practical, read on.

One simple rule, comprehensive enough to cover most contingencies, is this: Insert a comma wherever there is a *light natural pause.* Test it this way: Read your sentence aloud, in a measured voice, as if to a large audience. If you find that you naturally pause in a given place, or *must* pause to make the sense of your sentence instantly intelligible to the listener, insert a comma. Let your ear and good sense be your guides. If still in doubt, have a friend read the sentence aloud, slowly and emphatically. The pauses, if there are any, will begin announcing themselves.

Don't let yourself be intimidated by commas. Don't think you have to master 116 rules. Using commas correctly is mostly a matter of plain common sense. The rules simply codify what common sense recommends, and that's all. Even this business of being guided by your ear really boils down to common sense. Your "ear" tells you to pause in a given place because your mind—if it's alert—tells you that a pause there is appropriate. Instinctively you know that without that pause, the words would sound garbled.

I'll prove this by examining a basic rule. Read closely, please—only the first part will be boring. The rule: Whenever a conjunctive adverb such as *however, therefore, then,* or *besides* occurs in the interior of a sentence, it must be set off by commas BEFORE as well as after, or else by a semicolon and comma, depending on the nature of the sentence. The same rule applies to transitional expressions such as *for example, in fact, on the other hand, even so.* Read the following examples aloud and listen for the pauses:

   a You will agree, however, that Wagner's music is better than it sounds.

   b She is old enough to see her parents' faults; however, she is not old enough to forgive them.

In example *a*, many students would mistakenly omit the comma before *however*. That mistake, though, is analogous to setting off a parenthetical remark by a single parenthesis instead of a pair of them, one at each end. Note that *however* clearly interrupts the flow of the sentence; hence it is clearly parenthetical and must be set off by itself. One comma simply won't do the job. It's common sense.

In example *b*, many students would mistakenly use a comma instead of a semicolon before *however*. They would do so out of a failure to realize that the sentence consists of two independent clauses —two separate ideas, in other words. Observe that we come to a virtual full stop after *faults;* we then resume with a new, complete thought beginning *however*. If you were to substitute a comma for the semicolon before *however*, how would your reader know which clause *however* belongs with? Plainly, he wouldn't know. Only a semicolon (or a period) would tell him. Again, punctuating properly is a matter of common sense.

I have two last remarks to make about commas. The first concerns what is known as the "serial comma." The other concerns what are known as "comma splices." Both further confirm my point that punctuation is largely a matter of common sense.

Opinion is divided on whether to use a comma before the last item in a list or series. Should one write "apples, pears and peaches" or should one write "apples, pears, and peaches"? Both are acceptable, but experience shows that the latter is definitely preferable. Why? Because the final comma will eliminate any ambiguity that would necessitate a rereading of the sentence. There's no ambiguity, of course, with so simple a series as "apples, pears and peaches," particularly when it's just sitting there detached from context; but the more complex the series, the more likelihood there is of ambiguity. The beauty of that final comma before *and* is that it serves as a clear, instantaneous signal to your reader that he has reached the last item in the series. Without that final comma, the reader may not be able to determine what you mean, or else may be unwittingly seduced into a misreading. The sentence below is just such a teaser:

The prisoners in that cell included an unemployed actor, a murderer, a junkie, a man obsessed with flying saucers, an Indian millionaire with a constant craving for waffles and assorted females—all of them coexisting in surprising harmony.

Are the "assorted females" among the prisoners, or are they only on the mind of the Indian millionaire? We'll never know.

Consider, too, that most careful writers, habituated to using that final comma themselves, always expect to see it in the prose they read. When they find it absent, they become momentarily disoriented and irritated. So be prudent: learn to insert that comma as a matter of course.

And finally a word about "comma splices." Most of us have encountered the term, but few recall precisely what it refers to. A comma splice is a grammatical fault occurring whenever two independent clauses are connected by a mere comma. Example:

Bob wanted to leave early, he had a date that night.

Note that what we have here amounts to two sentences joined by a frail comma. An error such as this often occurs when a writer knows the relation between two thoughts in his own mind but neglects to show it to the reader. To repair the error, we need only add a coordinating conjunction right after the comma, or replace the comma with a strong semicolon, or break the two clauses into separate sentences, or recast the sentence. Examples:

a Bob wanted to leave early, for he had a date that night.
b Bob wanted to leave early; he had a date that night.
c Bob wanted to leave early. He had a date that night.
d Since he had a date that night, Bob wanted to leave early.

Parentheses

Parentheses give you a way of muscling into a sentence a piece of incidental information which you can't fit in grammatically, or which you don't want to bother to fit in grammatically, or which you want to de-emphasize because it amounts to a little footnote. Example:

That second trip to France (the one I told you about earlier) cost $410 but it was well worth it.

Use parentheses sparingly—for occasional variety, or where the need is compelling. They quickly become an eyesore, and no reader enjoys being repeatedly whispered to. If you *have* to use them, keep your insertions brief so that they don't overwhelm the rest of the sentence as this one does:

> Sir Harvey's most recent book (it originally came out in 1974 in Great Britain under the title of *All You Ever Wanted to Know About Me But Were Afraid to Inquire*) met with disquieting apathy, here as well as abroad.

One commonly misunderstood rule concerning parentheses is the following: A parenthetical insertion should be treated as part of the immediately *preceding* clause. Thus, if that clause requires a final comma or period, suspend it until after the parenthetical remark. Example:

> "OK, we're settled on 'All in the Family' as the title," the network executive replied, finally agreeing (though half in spite of himself), "but I really do draw the line on calling the guy Oedipus. I think we can come up with a more American name than that."

In essence, this rule is saying: Never punctuate immediately before a parenthesis. Always wait until *after*. The reason: parenthetical insertions don't want to be left hanging out there in limbo.

But suppose a parenthetical remark is to stand as a separate sentence? In that case, put the punctuation mark *inside* the parenthesis. (This sentence is an example.)

Dashes

If you understand that one may overuse a good thing, if you have attained a reasonably good grasp of commas and parentheses, and if you are interested in adding more verve to your style, then I recommend that you begin experimenting with the dash.

The dash, comma, and parenthesis are sister marks belonging to the family of Separators. Each of them sets off parenthetical matter. The comma handles all the routine chores such as this:

> But George, who hadn't had lessons, was as graceful as a dog on its hind legs.

The parenthesis takes over when some incidental information—an explanation or amplification—wants to be slipped into the sentence in the form of a low-voiced aside, or when it is not grammatically part of the sentence and so must be walled off from it. For example:

> This letter (a copy is enclosed) explains the School Board's position.

The dash, meanwhile, the most dramatic and spirited of the three, boldly steps in when the parenthetical matter wants to be set off for *emphasis,* or when there is to be a sudden break in the flow of the sentence.

Actually, the dash is so versatile and so eager to work that it occasionally moonlights as a colon, as a trailing-off thought ("If I could only—"), as a censor ("Oh, d——!"), and other such things. Unfortunately, novice writers instinctively recognize this trait and work it silly, asking it to double as a comma, a semicolon, a parenthesis, a period, *ad scandalam.* This is why it is tagged as a mark of Easy Virtue by many staid writers, who don't let it near their prose. Such an overreaction is a pity, really, because when the dash errs, it is a victim, not a culprit, and nothing can quite replace it.

Here are five things that the dash can do particularly well:

1 Mark an interruption or break in thought:

> Life without romance—well, you might as well be in a prison or a slug under the earth.—CHARLIE CHAPLIN

> To be middle-aged is to be—well, *what* is it? It is to have hope without expectation, courage without strength, desire without the fire.—H. L. MENCKEN

2 Serve as a conversational colon or light bridge:

Furthermore, recent discoveries in the physiology of the brain suggest that there may be two different kinds of intelligence—analytic, conceptual, verbal intelligence, located in the left hemisphere of the brain, and intuitive, artistic intelligence in the right hemisphere.
—*Newsweek*

That's the worst of facts—they do cramp a fellow's style.—C. S. LEWIS

Deadly, deflating accuracy is Sheed's game—the art of the neatly nipped hope.—MELVIN MADDOCKS

Sorry for the exclamation mark—I know how much you loathe the over-punctuation of under-thought frivolity.—GALE HICKMAN

3 Isolate a phrase—usually a concluding one—for emphasis or humorous effect:

The Dow Jones industrial average plummeted nearly 52 points in a week—the worst break in years.—*Time*

Fashion is illusion, shimmer, magic, mirage—and money: $62.3 billion a year.—SHANA ALEXANDER

Fame creates its own standards. A guy who twitches his lips is just another guy with a lip twitch—unless he's Humphrey Bogart.
—SAMMY DAVIS, JR.

I could never learn to like her—except on a raft at sea with no other provisions in sight.—MARK TWAIN

It's a naive, domestic burgundy—with absolutely no breeding—but I think you'll be amused by its presumption.—JAMES THURBER

4 Insert an important parenthetical explanation, qualification, or amplification:

Many of the wars fought by man—I am tempted to say most—have been fought over such abstractions. The more I puzzle over the great wars of history the more I am inclined to the view that the causes attributed to them—territory, markets, resources, the defense or perpetuation of great principles—were not the causes at all but rather explanations or excuses for certain unfathomable drives of human nature.—J. WILLIAM FULBRIGHT

IQ tests—and the academic establishment built upon the assumptions about the supreme value of conceptual intelligence—do not measure right-brain intelligence, much less such other vital performance factors as emotional understanding and patience.—*Newsweek*

5 Mark a gathering up of several ideas, often a series of subjects:

The art of the surprise witness, the withering cross-examination, the sudden objection phrased in arcane formulas—all seem to bespeak a profession based on elaborate training and requiring consummate skill.—*Time*

What these examples show, I think, is the remarkable way the dash animates a sentence. (The dash is aptly named. One meaning of the word is "animation in style and action," as in the phrase, "He cut a dashing figure.") Journalists have long recognized this; it explains why we encounter the mark so frequently in weekly news-magazines like *Newsweek* and *Time*. The staff writers of those maga-zines face the challenge of making week-old stories newly interesting —which is to say, dramatic. For this purpose the dash is almost indispensable. It's intrinsically dramatic and graphic.

There are four additional reasons, though, why good journalists rely on the dash. Since they have some pertinence to general writing as well, you ought to be aware of them:

a A long column of type can look forbiddingly heavy and black unless it's relieved by occasional dashes, which lighten it up and offer variety for the eye.

b When nothing but commas are used to set off modifying phrases, the commas tend to pile up quickly and clog one's sentences. The dash helps to relieve the congestion, not to mention the monotony.

c   Dashes are useful as an italics-substitute for calling attention to a key word or phrase. They dramatize it by setting it off at a distance and leading the eye right up to it. As a result, the reader can't run over it mentally the way he could if a mere comma were setting it off.

d   Dashes are also useful as a substitute for colons. Whereas the colon sometimes looks heavy and staid, the dash looks light, quick, and conversational. It seems virtually to move on the page because it has the effect of moving the reader's eye laterally.

A few last points and then we're done.

First, dashes come in two varieties: the *single* dash (used to set off something for emphasis, as at the end of a sentence) and the *double* dash (a *pair* of dashes used for inserting parenthetical matter). The two marks look exactly the same except that the double dash comes in a set, like parentheses. I'm only pointing this out to caution you against using both the single and the double dash in the same sentence. You'll simply confuse your reader, and your prose will look like chopped carrots. The example below illustrates the confusion. Here, the first two dashes are a double dash and the third is a single dash:

Just as Sam wearily finished writing his term paper—it had taken him nearly two months—he learned that he had missed the final deadline —by one hour.

Actually, it's a good idea to rest the dash for three or more sentences after each use. If you overuse it, it will lose its effect; in fact, it will begin looking gimmicky, and your reader may wonder whether you know how to write without it.

Second, never use a comma alongside a dash, even if the syntax seems to require it. The dash always works alone. If the syntax insists, the dash will silently absorb the work of the comma.

Finally, while the dash is printed in books as one long line, it is typed as *two consecutive hyphens* (with no space at either end) to distinguish it from the simple hyphen. This convention--illustrated here by arrangement with the typesetter--arose to meet the need of those many writers whose typewriters are not equipped with a special key for the dash. Don't type a little hyphen when you mean a dash.

Colons

As we saw earlier, the semicolon is used to join related thoughts while still preserving some separation between them—like this:

> The first half of life consists of the capacity to enjoy life without the chance; the last half consists of the chance without the capacity.
> —MARK TWAIN

The colon also joins related thoughts. However, it is used only when the first thought acts as an introduction or prelude to the second. If your first clause is waiting to be *explained,* or *particularized,* or in some way *completed,* then you will want to drop in a colon and proceed to give your reader what you have primed him to hear. In the example below, the second clause gives us all three things simultaneously:

> Girls have an unfair advantage over men: if they can't get what they want by playing smart, they can get it by playing dumb.
> —YUL BRYNNER

Note that here the colon is roughly equivalent to *that is* or *namely,* which are its typical implied meanings. Sometimes a writer will want to spell that out, using either of those phrases in conjunction with the colon:

> Nothing else is so likely to teach us what at this moment we most need to learn: namely, that more things can be actually *said* than we seem to believe and that so far as prose at least is concerned the best is that whose texture is firmly denotative and which can, as statement, stand firm on its own legs.—JOSEPH WOOD KRUTCH

In such cases as this, the colon really isn't necessary; a comma before and after *namely* would be equally grammatical. The sentence is a long one, though, and Mr. Krutch apparently decided that his reader would welcome more of a rest station than the first comma would have provided. I think he was right.

The basic use of the colon, then, is to signify *that is* or *namely*. The colon is also used, though, to introduce a list or series, at which time its meaning is *the following* or *as follows*. Here again a writer can spell it out, using the phrase as well as the colon, or simply let the colon do the job alone—like this:

The best methods of combatting organized crime are:
1. Telling the criminals you are not at home.
2. Calling the police whenever an unusual number of men from the Sicilian Laundry Company begin singing in your foyer.
3. Wiretapping.　　　　　　　　　　　　　　　—WOODY ALLEN

Below is a miscellany of additional examples. They will teach you the use of the colon much more quickly and painlessly than a set of abstract rules. Please observe that in most of the examples, the colon functions as a slightly more formal version of the dash. It tends to ready the mind to receive the completion of the thought begun in the initial clause:

Examining love is like examining a stocking: if you hold it up to the light and stretch it to search for snags, any snags there are may well run and ruin the stocking.—JO COUDERT

We need an alternative which is as challenging, emotionally exciting, as dramatic as war—and we have one now: rebuilding the cities, making war on our old prejudices (this war is in man's skull), and defeating poverty.—JOHN W. GARDNER

As an originator, powered by extraordinary energy of mind, Freud was capable of great forward bounds, so that he habitually extrapolated a whole system from a single item: saw the ocean in a drop of water, perceived a law of human behavior in a dropped handkerchief.—BARBARA TUCHMAN

Fields' very appearance evoked shouts of laughter from an audience: the manorial air that was so obviously false, the too benign smile, the larcenous eye.—COREY FORD

I make a sharp distinction between two kinds of concentration: one is immediate and complete, the other is plodding and only completed by stages.—STEPHEN SPENDER

The vision behind this book is simple and horrifying: it is the vision of the humanely educated Nazi.—ELIOT FREMONT-SMITH

Reading Eric Hoffer's *True Believer*, I noticed he had the same problem of resolution: he had trouble making all those ideas jell, so he put them down in their atomic form, almost like Euclid's axioms, and the result is very readable; and I can think of many other writers who would profit by excising pseudo transitions and the non-existent nexus.—WILLIAM FANKBONER

Here are a few other points you should know:

1 The colon is used to introduce a quotation when the quotation is longer than a single sentence or when it illustrates the point made in your lead-in clause. (See the section in the next chapter on "Punctuation introducing quotations.")

2 If the clause which follows your colon is a complete sentence, the first word of it may be capitalized or not, depending on the degree of emphasis you desire.

3 To avoid confusion, don't use more than one colon per sentence. For the same reason, you would be well advised not to allow a semicolon to follow a colon. The last example quoted above ignores this guideline, as you may have noticed, but it very rarely works successfully. That sentence happens to be one of those exceptional cases.

Exclamation points

"Screamers" in newspapermen's parlance, exclamation points are generally to be avoided for four reasons:

1 Since they are most often used by novice writers given to cuteness, exaggeration, and melodramatic effects, they have a bad odor to mature readers.

2 Many people prefer quiet, understated humor to the trumpeted, self-approving variety.

3 If the witticism is a fine one, it will hardly need an "Applause" sign to elicit the desired response. By the same token, if the witticism is a feeble one, the reader will resent being coerced to applaud it.

4 Sophisticated writers realize that omitting the exclamation point is a form of self-protection or insurance. If the witticism is good, they will be admired for the urbane dryness of their sense of humor. If the witticism misfires, the reader has no evidence convicting them of having even intended to be witty.

The exclamation point *must* be used, however, after true exclamations or commands. Examples: "What a predicament!" "How glacial she is!" "Stop!"

Quotation marks

Set off a word or phrase by quotation marks when making reference to it or when using it in a special sense (e.g., technically, humorously, ironically). Thus:

A more recent instance of double-think was our practice of calling the war in Viet Nam a "conflict."

"Puritanism," as defined by H. L. Mencken, is "the haunting fear that someone, somewhere, may be happy."

Many people mistakenly think that "imply" and "infer" are synonyms.

Is this holocaust what you mean by "pacification"?

A helpful tip offered by Ken Macrorie in his excellent book, *Telling Writing*, is this: "More often than not, the words *say, call, refer to as* are followed by quoted words." One might add to that list *the word* and *the words*. Macrorie's own sentence illustrates the point.

For extra emphasis, or when a number of words are being cited, substitute underlining for quotation marks. Underlining translates typographically as italics.

One further point which probably ought to be set in bold capitals: If you ever use a cliché, never—repeat *never*—put it in quotation marks, as in the following example:

His wooden dullness indicated that he was indeed a "chip off the old block."

Two reasons justify the stringent prohibition: (1) quotation marks only serve to compound your offense by drawing added attention to the trite expression; and (2) they irritate the reader because, implicitly, you are telling him that you really know better. If you really did know better, why use the cliché in the first place?

Hyphens

Compound adjectives are always hyphenated, the reason being that the two (or more) words that compose them make sense adjectivally only when understood as components of a single, complex adjective. Study the following examples well and you'll soon develop a sense for when the hyphen is required:

eighteenth-century painting; ear-jarring sounds; triple-option offense; three-base hit; so-called neurosis; twelve-year-old boy; well-known speaker

There is one exception to this rule, however, which you should make a serious effort to remember since it occurs frequently. Look again at the last example in the group above: "well-known speaker." Here the adjective phrase is composed of an adverb and a verb. *Whenever the adverb ends in "-ly," the hyphen is dropped.* Examples:

widely known speaker; sensibly tailored suit; firmly held opinion; sharply reduced prices

Two last points. First, few students seem to realize that whenever *self* is used as a prefix, it must be followed by a hyphen. Examples:

self-confidence; self-esteem; self-made; self-denial; self-taught; self-preservation

Second, "suspension" hyphens are always used whenever the parts of compound words get separated from each other. Examples:

The pre- and post-game shows were equally dull.

In second- and third-down situations, Coach Murphy usually sends in a pass-option play.

13 Conventions regarding quotations

Are you confused by this? You look confused . . . amused . . . or maybe a little repulsed.

J. V. FLEMING

1. Punctuation introducing quotations

Use a *comma* whenever your quotation is short and when you've introduced it with a phrase such as "he said," "he replied." Example:

> Twain observed, "Only presidents, editors, and people with tapeworms have the right to use the editorial 'we.' "

In almost all other situations, however, use a *colon.* Three of the commonest situations requiring a colon are these: (a) when you have made a statement and now wish to bring in a quote* to illustrate it or amplify it; (b) when your quote exceeds a single sentence or two typed lines; and (c) when you plan to indent your quote because of its length. The first two of these situations are illustrated below, while the third situation will be illustrated later with the final example under item #5:

---

* A formidable 85% of *The American Heritage Dictionary*'s Usage Panel considered the noun *quote* to be unacceptable as a substitute for *quotation.* I will side with the enlightened minority here—and with George Orwell ("Never use a long word where a short one will do")—though I will occasionally use *quotation* where it won't overtax the sentence. *Quote* is shorter by two syllables, is idiomatic, and is always clear in context.

Twain's pose as a connoisseur of good breeding allowed him to speak solemnly of the ridiculous: "Miss C. B. had her fine nose elegantly enameled, and the easy grace with which she blew it from time to time marked her as a cultivated and accomplished woman of the world; its exquisitely modulated tone excited the admiration of all who had the happiness to hear it."

James Thurber remarked: "Word has somehow got around that the split infinitive is always wrong. This is of a piece with the outworn notion that it is always wrong to strike a lady."

Frequently you won't want to quote an entire sentence since only a phrase or clause may be really pertinent. At such times, simply incorporate what you need of the quote right into the mainstream of your sentence, treating the phrase or clause as if it were your own. No introductory punctuation is necessary unless the syntax of your sentence requires it. Example:

Mencken said that *Comrades* "will lie embalmed in my memory as a composition unearthly and unique—as a novel without a single redeeming merit."

2. Punctuation at end of quotations

Most stylistic conventions make sense. You may have to think about them a little, but eventually you'll find a satisfying, logical rationale behind them. A few conventions, though, are so illogical as to seem downright perverse. One of these is the very basic rule governing punctuation at the end of quotations. It states: *Commas and periods always go INSIDE closing quotation marks, even if the comma or period was not part of the original quotation.*

Fortunately, the corollary to this rule returns us to the world of reason. It states: *Colons and semicolons always go OUTSIDE closing quotation marks.*

Remembering these rules is hard, even though every published piece of writing that we read gives us daily illustrations of them.

Here, though, are two more examples. If you stare at them long enough, what looks wrong will eventually look right:

He said "bed," not "wed."

Oscar Wilde remarked, "Truth is never pure, and rarely simple"; half-truths, however, suffer neither of these inconveniences and thus have always proved more popular.

Frequently a student, confused about these rules, will strike what he hopes is an ingenious and happy compromise—or, failing that, something that he prays the reader will charitably construe as a slip of the typing finger. The "solution" involves placing the comma or period directly *under* the closing quotation mark. Resourceful as this may be, it is, alas, akin to observing a yellow light by coming to a stop midway through the intersection.

3. Indented quotations

Long quotations should be typed single-spaced and indented moderately from both the right and left margins. This practice greatly enhances their readability because the reader, able to determine the length of the quote at a glance, is relieved of the anxiety that he might overlook the closing quotation mark.

Normally, prose quotations are indented when they begin to get bulky—say, at 4–5 lines. Verse quotations, on the other hand, are normally indented when they exceed 2 lines. Make sure that in both cases you *omit* quotation marks since indenting serves the same purpose as quotation marks and thus makes them redundant.

Indented quotes are usually introduced with a *colon*. Occasionally, though, you may be able to make the quote fit grammatically into the mainstream of your sentence. In such cases, no introductory punctuation is necessary unless the syntax of your sentence requires it. Example:

The problem, Fulbright says, is that

> power tends to confuse itself with virtue, and a great nation is
> peculiarly susceptible to the idea that its power is a sign of
> God's favor, conferring upon it a special responsibility for
> other nations—to make them richer and happier and wiser, to
> remake them, that is, in its own shining image.

Novice writers commonly make two mistakes with indented quotations. The first is to introduce an indented quote with a lead-in comment ending in a period instead of the normal colon. You can see, with a little thought, why it is so important to use the colon. If you were to terminate your lead-in with a period, the quotation would hang below it, unattached, in a kind of syntactical limbo. Your confused reader would be asking himself, "Is the quote meant to illustrate the comment immediately preceding it, or will the commentary immediately follow it?" Using a colon will clearly tie your quote to the statement it pertains to.

The second common mistake is to sandwich an indented quotation between the beginning and ending parts of a sentence. Example:

In 1922, while observing the behavior of hens and ducks, the
Norwegian Schjelderup-Ebbe noticed a distinct "pecking order"
among them:

> In any small flock of hens there soon develops a rather firmly
> fixed hierarchy, in which the top hen normally has the right to
> peck all the others without being pecked in return: and each
> of the others occupies a place subordinate to hers, usually in a
> linear series with respect to one another down to the lowest
> bird, which all may peck without fear of retaliation.

and ever since that time anthropologists have applied the term to the hierarchy of dominance observed among humans as well.

This practice of sandwiching quotes is ill-advised for two reasons: first, it almost always forces a rereading of the entire sentence, quotation and all, since by the time one gets to the conclusion of the sentence, one has forgotten how it began; and second, the practice will usually be found to be ungrammatical since most quotes end in a period which automatically terminates the sentence then and there.

In summary, follow these guidelines:

a Set up each indented quote with a lead-in ending in a colon, and let the quote terminate the sentence.

b So that your reader will be able to make full sense of the quote on a single reading, offer your major comments first and *then* bring in the quote to illustrate those comments. This puts the horse before the cart where it belongs.

4. Punctuating run-on quotations of poetry

Verse quotations of two lines or less should be run on, in quotation marks, as part of your text so as to conserve space. Be sure, however, to use a *slash* (/) to indicate the end of one line and the beginning of the next. Also, begin each new line with a capital letter unless the poet himself has done otherwise. Example:

In his characterization of Belinda, Alexander Pope pays the supreme tribute to the power of beauty: "If to her share some Female Errors fall, / Look on her Face, and you'll forget 'em all" (*The Rape of the Lock,* II.17–18).

5. References for quotations

For the convenience of your reader, you should specify the page reference (or line reference, if the lines are numbered) for each quotation.

One way to specify a reference, of course, is with the conventional footnote. The initial footnote to a book or article typically specifies all of the following: author, title, city of publication, publisher, date of publication, and page number of the quotation. Example:

[1] Northrop Frye, *Anatomy of Criticism: Four Essays* (Princeton, N.J.: Princeton Univ. Press, 1957), p. 31.

Subsequent references to that source typically specify merely the author's name and page number. Example: Frye, p. 32. (For answers to any questions you may have concerning other aspects of footnoting procedure, consult either the *MLA Style Sheet,* available at most campus bookstores, or *A Manual of Style,* published by The University of Chicago Press.)

In recent years, however, what with the flood of highly specialized scholarly works that we've been drowning in, more and more writers have come to see footnotes as odious. They are distracting to the reader; they are a nuisance to type; they smack of unreadable research papers; they are a waste of space. As a result, footnotes are now beginning to be used more as a last resort than as a matter of course. In place of them, writers are now learning to use "parenthetical references"—i.e., *brief references supplied in parentheses immediately following their quotations.* This has become the preferred form especially whenever most of the quotations are drawn from the same work.

This simplified form has itself undergone additional simplification during the past decade. More and more writers are now putting *merely the number* of the page or line in parentheses, provided that the number is unambiguous. For example, instead of writing "(p. 200)," you would write simply "(200)." Should confusion be likely, however, you must exercise one of these two options: (a) explain in a footnote to your first quotation that page (or line) references will hereafter be given parenthetically in the text—after which you can go ahead and use simply the numbers in parentheses; or (b) use these abbreviations: *p.* for *page* and *l.* for *line.* (The plural forms are *pp.* and *ll.*)

The procedure for references to plays deserves special explanation. If you have occasion to give a line reference to a play by Shakespeare, you have a choice of forms for your parenthetical reference: (II.ii.553), (II.2.553), (2.2.553). Note that the last number in each of these examples refers to the line, not the page. Shakespeare's plays, remember, were written in blank verse; hence all the lines are numbered as in any long poem. Incidentally, when referring to a particular Act of a play, capitalize *Act* to distinguish the word from *act* (= action) and use capital roman numerals. Example: Act II. The word *scene* is not capitalized since there is no threat of ambiguity. If you are quoting from a non-Shakespearean play, it is usually sufficient to cite merely the Act and page number. Example: (III, 88).

We come now to the question of how to punctuate a parenthetical reference. Since this takes some getting used to, students commonly run into problems here, so read attentively. There are only two rules to remember. First, the parenthetical reference should be treated as part of the clause in which your quotation is given; thus the final punctuation of that clause will come *after* the parenthetical reference. Second, *omit* any punctuation originally at the end of your quote since it is now nonfunctional and would result in ungrammatical double-punctuation. In short, you *may* punctuate *after* a parenthetical reference but you may NOT punctuate before it. Sounds impossibly confusing, doesn't it? Well, if you study the following example, you'll see how very simple this procedure really is. Observe the absence of punctuation immediately preceding the parentheses:

When King Henry describes how, by being seldom seen, he managed to keep his presence "like a robe pontifical, / Ne'er seen but wonder'd at" (3.2.56–57), we hear telling echoes of Prince Hal's earlier words, "Being wanted, he may be more wonder'd at" (1.2.207).

Exceptions: Common sense will remind you that quotes ending with either an *exclamation point* or a *question mark* are necessary exceptions to the rule about no punctuation before a parenthesis. In such cases the punctuation is obviously essential to the sense of the quotation and thus must be retained within the quotes. This will often necessitate a second punctuation mark (i.e., your own) after the parenthetical reference. Example:

"Oh what a rogue and peasant slave am I!" (2.2.553), Hamlet exclaims.

References for indented quotations have their own procedure. It is even simpler than the one described above. First, end the quotation with whatever terminal punctuation applies. Then, *drop down one line* and set the parenthetical reference even with the indented right-hand margin of the quotation. This procedure will keep the quotation visually uncluttered and the indented margin unbroken. Example:

But literary criticism, for Mencken, was a fine art, not a science. And why? Because, to his staunchly unsentimental mind, criticism is finally "no more than prejudice made plausible" (62). He summed up his attitude thus:

> If the critic, retiring to his cell to concoct his treatise upon a book or play or what-not, produces a piece of writing that shows sound structure, and brilliant color, and the flash of new and persuasive ideas, and civilized manners, and the charm of an uncommon personality in free function, then he has given something to the world that is worth having, and sufficiently justified his existence.
> (102)

6. Ellipses

Ellipsis points, which consist of three *spaced* periods (. . .), are used to indicate an omission of a word or words in a quotation, most typically somewhere in the middle of it. Such an omission is called an "ellipsis" (pl., "ellipses"). If you are quoting an obvious fragment —e.g., a mere clause or phrase—ellipsis points are unnecessary. Indeed, they are an insult to the reader, who can see for himself that you have omitted something. But if you think a failure to indicate an ellipsis might *seriously* mislead the reader, you should insert the spaced periods. Practically speaking, though, keep in mind that ellipsis points are actually rarely needed and should be used sparingly. They quickly become an eyesore. This point can't be overstressed.

Note: If you end your sentence with a quotation that has an ellipsis at the end, you must supply a final punctuation mark. The ellipsis, while written as three spaced periods, does not double as a period. Example:

> Mme. Geoffrin remarked of her grandmother, "She spoke so pleasantly about things she did not know, that no one wished she knew more about them. . . ."

In the original, a comma follows the word *them*. Convention allows that comma (or any other punctuation mark) to be silently deleted since the ellipsis indicates an omission anyway. Observe, too, that whenever you have an ellipsis at the end of a sentence, there is no space between the last letter and the first of the four periods. Below is a sentence containing an ellipsis in the middle and at the end as well. Note the difference:

> His reply deserved being engraved on a stone tablet: "Writing is a difficult art . . . because it involves thinking logically and interestingly, two operations which are unnatural to most of our minds. . . ."

Note also: Ellipsis points at the beginning of a quotation are visually distracting and, more often than not, easily avoided. Simply merge the abbreviated quotation with an apt introductory clause so that the two are syntactically continuous. The initial letter of the quotation, being written in lowercase, will immediately signal your reader that the quote is truncated:

> Jacques Barzun neatly summed up the importance of clarity with his remark that "a written exercise is designed to be read; it is not supposed to be a challenge to clairvoyance."

Note further: If, in quoting a passage of verse, you wish to omit one or more whole lines, simply type an entire line of consecutive, spaced periods to indicate a substantial omission. Your parenthetical reference at the end of the quote will allow the reader to determine the extent of the omission: he can simply subtract the number of lines you've actually quoted from the total of the lines you've given in the parentheses.

One last point. If you are writing dialogue and want to express a thought that is trailing off, use three spaced periods instead of the customary four at the end of the sentence, and skip a space before the first of those periods. Example: "It isn't that I don't love you but . . ."

7. Editorial insertions (square brackets)

This is another form of tampering with quotations. It consists of an insertion (by you) of an explanatory word or phrase inside a quotation. Don't make the common mistake of inserting the interjection in parentheses, since your reader would then obviously have no way of identifying the insertion as yours. Instead, always use *brackets*. If your typewriter is not equipped with them, and most aren't, simply write them in. Example:

George Eliot says of Dorothea, "she felt that she enjoyed it [horseback-riding] in a pagan sensuous way, and always looked forward to renouncing it" (*Middlemarch*, I.i).

14 *Tips on usage*

Good writers are those who keep the language efficient. That is to say, keep it accurate, keep it clear.

abbreviations Below are some common abbreviations, most of them used chiefly in footnotes where conserving space is important. Avoid using them freely in the body of your text—you'll risk looking either pedantic or lazy, plus you'll risk needlessly confusing your reader, who may not be familiar with the apparatus of scholarly writing. The Latin abbreviations in this list are followed by the complete Latin word or phrase from which they are derived. In times past, writers underlined (italicized) them to indicate their Latin derivation; current practice favors no underlining. For a more complete list of abbreviations, consult either *A Manual of Style* (The University of Chicago Press) or *The MLA Style Sheet*:

c., *circa,* about, approximately. It's used with dates. Example: "He was born **c.** 1820." *Circa* is occasionally also abbreviated "ca."

cf., *confer,* compare. Use "cf." only when you wish the reader to compare one thing with another. Example: "Cf. Monet's sketch of the same cathedral." Many novice writers mistakenly use "cf." when they mean "see" as in "See pp. 8–10 for a full discussion of this point."

chap., chapter

cont., continued

ed., edited by; edition; editor. The plural is "eds."

e.g., *exempli gratia,* for example. Use commas before and after it, just as you would if you were writing "for example," or else a dash before it and a comma after it. Example: "Conrad also employs this device in some of his short stories—e.g., 'The Secret Sharer.' "

et al., *et alii,* and others.   Example: "This essay was later anthologized in *Criticism,* ed. Mark Schorer et al." Since "et" is a complete Latin word, don't put a period after it—a common mistake.

etc., *et cetera,* and so forth.   Frequently, novice writers mistakenly write "and etc." or "etc., etc." Both are redundancies. "Etc." is preceded by a comma.

f., and the following page or line.   The plural is "ff." Example: "His notebooks quoted on p. 23 f. and p. 60 ff. touch on these same issues." Observe that a space follows each numeral. In the interest of exactness, it's best to avoid this lazy man's abbreviation; instead, specify the final number as well as the first. Example: "His notebooks quoted on pp. 23–24 and pp. 60–66 touch on these same issues."

ibid., *ibidem,* in the same place.   "Ibid." is used in footnotes to specify the same title as the one cited in the immediately preceding note. If the page reference as well as the title remains the same, "ibid." alone is sufficient. If the page reference is different, you must specify it. Example: " ² Ibid., p. 42."

i.e., *id est,* that is.   As with "e.g.," this abbreviation is set off by commas fore and aft, or, in some cases, by a dash and a comma. Example: "The titles of books, however, must be underlined, i.e., set in italics."

l., line.   The plural is "ll." Since this abbreviation can easily be confused with the arabic numeral 1, it's best to avoid it. You'll spare your reader sentences like, "A less complete statement of Eliot's theme appears in ll. 11–13."

l.c., lowercase

MS, manuscript.   The plural is "MSS." A period after "MS" is optional, but current usage favors dispensing with it.

N.B., *nota bene,* note well.   Example: "N.B.: this characterization was deleted in the original transcript."

op. cit., *opere citato,* in the work cited.   "Op. cit." is sometimes used in footnoting to eliminate the need for repeatedly writing out a long title. If you've already cited a work—say, Eugene O'Neill's *Long Day's Journey into Night*—you may now substitute "op. cit." for the title and give the new page reference. Example: " ⁸ O'Neill, op. cit., p. 40." A much clearer procedure, though, is to provide a shortened form of the title instead of "op. cit." Example: " ⁸ O'Neill, *Long Day's Journey,* p. 40."

p., page. The plural is "pp."

pub., published by

viz., *videlicet,* namely. Set it off by commas fore and aft.

vol., volume. The plural is "vols."

vs., *versus,* against, versus

all right *All right* is right; *alright* is wrong. So many people don't know *alright* is wrong, though, that in another decade or two it will probably be recognized as Standard English. And it deserves to be. It's a shorter form than *all right* and says exactly the same thing. Nothing would be lost except surplusage.

a lot It is written as two words, not one, but many readers would prefer you to remember not to write it at all—it's slangy. Oddly, though, its slanginess seems to vanish in certain contexts: it will be so appropriate that you won't even notice it, and if by chance you did, it would defy criticism. Flip back to the Updike passage which ends chapter 7 and you'll see what I mean. The typical alternatives —*many* and *much*—simply wouldn't work there. Conclusion: In cases such as this, your ear must be your sole guide.

and/or *And/or* is, to many readers, an unwieldy monstrosity associated with income-tax prose. Its sole virtue is brevity. Without it one would have to say "X or Y, or both"—itself something of an unwieldy monstrosity, in my opinion.

assure — ensure — insure All three words mean "to make certain or safe." Use *assure* with persons, *ensure* with things, and *insure* when talking about money and guarantees (e.g., life insurance).

between — among When speaking of just two persons or things, use *between*; of three or more, use *among*. If a tight relationship is implied, though, use *between* regardless of the number. Examples: "The quarrel between Mike, Jim, and Larry is still raging"; "The flights between London, Geneva, and Berlin have been canceled."

cannot   *Cannot* is the preferred way to write *can not*. Experienced writers save *can not* for those rare situations where they want to put special emphasis on the word *not*.

consensus   The word means "collective opinion" or "general agreement." Since it already includes the idea of opinion, the phrase *consensus of opinion* is redundant. Likewise with *the general consensus*. Simply say, for example, "The consensus is that the bill will pass the Senate."

criterion — criteria   You can have but one *criterion*. However, you can have two or more *criteria*. Moral: Don't use *criteria* when you're speaking of only one thing. (It's a common error.) Here are some allied words: *medium* and *media, memorandum* and *memoranda, datum* and *data, stratum* and *strata*.

different from — different than   Since one thing differs *from* another, say *different from* except where it creates a cumbersome or wordy clause after it, in which case *different than* is not only acceptable but preferable.

disinterested — uninterested   If you are *disinterested*, you are unbiased or impartial. If you are *uninterested*, you are not interested. The difference in meaning between the two words is so radical that it's worth making a special point of remembering which is which.

factor   Doesn't it have a lovely scientific ring to it? This probably explains why it appears with such depressing frequency in undergraduate writing. We really ought to put a 10-year moratorium on this word. We could get along perfectly well with its synonyms: *component, ingredient, element*.

famous — notorious   If a person is widely known and acclaimed, he is *famous*. But if a person is widely known because he is disreputable, he is *notorious* (infamous).

first — firstly   In enumerating several items, say *first*, not *firstly*. The reasons: *first* is as genuine an adverb as *firstly*, is a simpler form, and is much more natural to the ear. The same applies to *second, third, fourth*, etc. Occasionally you may decide that the numerals themselves are preferable to the words, as in this example from Twain: "To be a writer, one must observe three rules: (1) write, (2) write, and (3) write." Note that the numerals are enclosed on both sides by parentheses. Note, too, that a comma plus *and* precedes the final numeral. When the enumerated items are each quite lengthy, substitute semicolons for the commas to enhance readability.

imply — infer These words are commonly confused. If someone (such as an author) has *implied* something, he has hinted it or intimated it instead of saying it outright; if someone else (such as a reader) gets the hint, he has *inferred* it—that is, deduced the veiled point. The difference is thus analogous to that between giving and receiving something.

irregardless If you use the word, you actually mean *regardless.* Technically we can't call *irregardless* a nonword, for there it is, but it deserves to be a nonword since the suffix *less* makes the prefix *ir* plainly redundant. In any case, it's "nonstandard."

its — it's Here's another pair of commonly confused words. *It's* is the contraction of *it is,* whereas *its* is the possessive form of *it.* Normally, of course, possession is indicated by the apostrophe. In this case it isn't, because *its* belongs to a special class of words known as prenominal or "pure" possessives. Other words like it include *hers, theirs, yours, ours.* None of these uses the apostrophe.

like — as If there's a verb following it, use *as.* If not, use *like.* The famous Winston ad, for example, should have read, "Winston tastes good, as a cigarette should." Compare to "Molly dresses like her sister."

loathe — loath You may *loathe* a bad habit, yet still be *loath* (unwilling) to give it up.

loose — lose If a button is *loose,* you are apt to *lose* it.

neither It's followed by *nor,* not *or.* Example: "Neither Bill nor his father ate the turnips with relish." Use *or* only with *either.*

none *None* confuses most people. Is it singular or plural? The answer is that it can be either. If it is followed by a singular noun, it is construed as singular; if by a plural noun, it is construed as plural. Thus:

None of the building was painted.
None of the guests were here when I arrived.

If no noun follows it, simply decide whether you are talking about more than one and pick your verb accordingly. If you wish to give special emphasis to the fact of singleness, though, substitute *no one* or *not one*. Thus: "Not one of his shots touched the rim."

only   Make sure you put it immediately before the word it actually modifies. Compare these two sentences:

Sam only plays golf on weekends.
Sam plays golf only on weekends.

The first version implies that Sam does nothing each weekend except play golf—he doesn't mow the lawn, take the family on an outing, come home to eat, nothing. The second version implies that the only time Sam plays golf is on weekends.

precede   *Precede* ("to come before") is perhaps the most commonly misspelled word in student writing. It apparently gets confused with *proceed* and comes out misspelled as *preceed*.

principal — principle   If you're referring to a rule or basic truth, say *principle*. This word functions only as a noun. Its sound-alike, *principal,* denotes "chief" and can be used as either a noun or an adjective: e.g., "the principal of the school," "the principal witness." Don't feel alone if you always have to check the difference in the dictionary. Almost everyone does, I imagine.

¶   Although it offends one's sense of logic, the proofreader's symbol for a new paragraph is ¶, not ℙ.

reason is because   This is a redundancy. The reason is that *because* means *for the reason that.* Say one or the other, not both. Examples:

He double-parked because he was rushed.
The reason he double-parked is that he was rushed.

revert — regress   Both mean "to go back." Thus the colloquialisms "revert back" and "regress back" are redundancies. Simply say, for example, "He reverted to his old ways."

shall — will When your grandfather was in school, he was taught the vital difference in usage between these two words. But he forgot that difference along with nearly everybody else—apparently it wasn't so vital after all—and now the words are interchangeable. *Shall,* though, sounds slightly fussier and more bookish to the average ear, so if you're aiming at a conversational style, use *will* instead. The exception would be a first-person interrogative: "Shall we dance?" "Shall I pick her up at the station or will you?"

so Many people believe that *so* is an intensifier synonymous with *very* ("This coffee is so strong"). It is not, however. Observe that when you write a sentence such as the one just illustrated, your reader will unconsciously—and properly—expect a *that* clause to follow: "This coffee is so strong that I can't drink it."

there is — there are Both are dead phrases and should be used as a last resort. Eliminating them through recasting usually results in sentences that are more vivid, concrete, and terse. There are many exceptions, though, and this sentence is one of them.

thus *Thus* is an adverb. Many students, not realizing this, think they must attach to it the regular adverbial suffix *-ly* to have it function as an adverb. *Thusly,* however, is an illiteracy.

unique If a thing is *unique,* it's the only one of its kind. The condition is an absolute one, like perfection. Thus you can't logically talk about *unique* in terms of degree. You can't say, for example, "rather unique" or "the most unique" or "very unique." A thing is either unique or it is not unique, just as a woman is either pregnant or she is not pregnant. When writers misuse *unique,* they usually mean *unusual* or *rare.* "A rather unique invitation," for example, should read "a rather unusual invitation."

used to In conversation it's hard to hear that final *d,* but it's there—or should be, since it's the past participle of the verb *use* ("to be accustomed to"). Thus, say "I used to work there," not "I use to work there."

whether Use it alone. Don't tack on the redundancy *or not* as in the sentence, "He doesn't know whether or not to go." The *or not* is necessary only when you mean to convey the idea of *regardless of whether.* Example: "We're going to play golf today whether it rains or not."

15   *Epilog*

Some months ago I ran across a cartoon depicting a scene aboard a commercial airliner. As the startled passengers look on, the whole crew, outfitted in parachutes, strolls down the aisle towards the rear escape hatch. Leading them out is the pilot, his hands nonchalantly tucked in his pockets and a casual whistle on his guiltily upturned face.

I confess I see myself in that pilot. Here I am, cravenly parachuting out of harm's way on the wings of a final paragraph, and there you are, abandoned to your own devices just when the trip has started getting bumpy. I hope, though, that this book, brief as it is, has given you new insight into how skilled writers think, plus the itch to go out and write like them yourself. Writing well is hard work, but it can be *pleasant* hard work if we view it for what it really is—a challenge to our creativity, an opportunity to know our own mind, and a chance to share our thoughts and feelings with others. That's certainly what this book has meant for me. Thanks for listening.

List of sources

Note: Because I started collecting the quotations used in this book for personal reference only, long before the book itself was conceived, I occasionally neglected to record any source other than the author's name. I have managed to track down most of these fugitive quotations, but a few regretfully remain at large. Unattributed examples in the text are my own.

page

3 John Updike, in a commentary written for *On Writing, By Writers,* ed. William W. West (Lexington, Mass.: Ginn and Co., 1966), p. 121.

3 George Orwell, "Politics and the English Language," *Shooting an Elephant and Other Essays* (New York: Harcourt, Brace, 1950), p. 89.

5 Pauline Kael, *Deeper Into Movies* (Boston: Little, Brown, 1973), pp. 423, 316–17.

9 Peter Elbow, *Writing without Teachers* (New York: Oxford, 1973), p. 29.

10 James A. Michener, quoted in A. Grove Day, *James A. Michener* (New York: Twayne, 1964), p. 134.

12 Walter Pater, "Leonardo Da Vinci," *The Renaissance: Studies in Art and Poetry* (London: Macmillan, 1914), p. 103.

13 Ernest Hemingway, "Advice to a Young Man," *Playboy,* XI (January 1964), p. 153.

13 F. L. Lucas, *Style* (London: Cassell, 1955), p. 76.

18 Samuel Butler, *The Note-Books of Samuel Butler,* ed. Henry Festing Jones (London: A. C. Fifield, 1918), p. 329.

20 W. Somerset Maugham, *The Summing Up* (Garden City, N.Y.: Doubleday, 1938), pp. 30–31.

21 George M. Trevelyan, *Clio, a Muse and Other Essays Literary and Pedestrian* (London: Longmans, Green, 1913), p. 34.

21 James A. Michener, quoted in Day, *Michener,* p. 135.

21 E. B. White, quoted in Donald M. Murray, *A Writer Teaches Writing* (Boston: Houghton Mifflin, 1968), p. 245.

24 George Bernard Shaw, in *Ellen Terry and Bernard Shaw: A Correspondence,* ed. Christopher St. John (New York: The Fountain Press, 1931), p. 113.

25 Virginia Woolf, "The Modern Essay," *The Common Reader,* Harvest Book ed. (New York: Harcourt, Brace, 1953), p. 227.

27 W. H. Auden, *The Dyer's Hand and Other Essays* (New York: Random House, 1962), p. 8.

29 Kael, *Deeper Into Movies,* p. 219.

30 Wendell Berry, "Some Thoughts I Have in Mind When I Teach," *Writers as Teachers. Teachers as Writers,* ed. Jonathan Baumbach (New York: Holt, Rinehart and Winston, 1970), p. 23.

30 John Mason Brown, *Dramatis Personae: A Retrospective Show,* Compass Book ed. (New York: Viking, 1965), p. 458.

37 H. L. Mencken, quoted in William H. Nolte, *H. L. Mencken: Literary Critic* (Middletown, Conn.: Wesleyan Univ. Press, 1966), p. 33.

46 George Bernard Shaw, "Epistle Dedicatory" prefacing *Man and Superman.*

55 Lucas, *Style,* pp. 39–40.

59 Donald Hall, *Writing Well* (Boston: Little, Brown, 1973), p. 42.

59 Sydney Smith, quoted in Lady Holland, *A Memoir of the Reverend Sydney Smith,* vol. 1 (New York: Harper & Brothers, 1856), p. 333.

61 Hemingway, "Advice to a Young Man," p. 153.

62 Theodore M. Bernstein, *The Careful Writer: A Modern Guide to Usage* (New York: Atheneum, 1965), p. 14.

64 Mark Twain, *Selected Shorter Writings of Mark Twain,* ed. Walter Blair (Boston: Houghton Mifflin, 1962), p. 226.

64 Elizabeth Taylor, *Elizabeth Taylor: An Informal Memoir* (New York: Harper & Row, 1965), p. 124.

64 John W. Aldridge, *Time to Murder and Create: The Contemporary Novel in Crisis* (New York: David McKay, 1966), p. 169.

64 T. S. Eliot, *On Poetry and Poets* (New York: Farrar, Straus and Cudahy, 1957), p. 111.

65 Theodor Seuss Geisel, quoted in Murray, *A Writer Teaches Writing,* p. 237.

65 Ford Madox Ford, *Joseph Conrad: A Personal ·Remembrance* (London: Duckworth, 1924), p. 197.

65 Ray Bradbury, "Seeds of Three Stories," in *On Writing, By Writers,* ed. West, p. 48.

66 Nolte, *Mencken,* p. 55.

66 Dwight Macdonald, *Against the American Grain* (New York: Random House, 1962), p. 192.

66   Charles W. Ferguson, *Say It with Words* (New York: Knopf, 1959), pp. 57–58. ·

67   H. L. Mencken, *Prejudices: First Series* (New York: Knopf, 1919), p. 12.

67   Brown, *Dramatis Personae*, p. 99.

67   Joseph Conrad, "Preface" to *The Nigger of the Narcissus.*

67   John Updike, "Upright Carpentry," in *Assorted Prose,* copyright © 1958 by John Updike (New York: Alfred A. Knopf, Inc., 1965), p. 77. Used with permission.

69   Blaise Pascal, *Pensées,* Section I, #29.

69   Robert Frost, "Preface" to *A Way Out* in *Robert Frost: Poetry and Prose,* ed. Edward C. Lathem and Lawrance Thompson (New York: Holt, Rinehart and Winston, 1972), pp. 272–73.

70   F. Scott Fitzgerald, *The Crack-up,* ed. Edmund Wilson, New Directions ed. (New York: James Laughlin, 1956), p. 69.

73   Orwell, "Politics and the English Language," pp. 85, 87.

73   James M. McCrimmon, *Writing with a Purpose* (Boston: Houghton Mifflin, 1972), p. 410.

73   Porter G. Perrin, *Writer's Guide and Index to English,* 3rd ed. (Chicago: Scott, Foresman, 1959), pp. 15–20.

74   Maugham, *The Summing Up,* p. 38.

74   Bonamy Dobrée, *Modern Prose Style,* 2nd ed. (Oxford: Clarendon, 1964), p. 218.

79   Mark Twain, "Pudd'nhead Wilson's Calendar," *Pudd'nhead Wilson,* ch. 11.

80   Henry Thoreau, *Walden. Where I Lived, and What I Lived For,* in *Walden and Other Writings of Henry David Thoreau,* ed. Brooks Atkinson (New York: Modern Library, 1950), p. 82.

80   W. Somerset Maugham, quoted in Cyril Connolly, *Enemies of Promise,* rev. ed. (New York: Macmillan, 1948), p. 35.

80   Hemingway, "Advice to a Young Man," p. 153.

81   Lucas, *Style,* p. 132.

83   e. e. cummings, *E. E. Cummings: A Miscellany,* ed. George J. Firmage (New York: Argophile, 1958), p. 13.

83   Donald Lloyd, "Snobs, Slobs, and the English Language," *The American Scholar,* XX (Summer 1951), p. 279.

88   Robert Frost, "Introduction" to *King Jasper* by Edward Arlington Robinson.

88   Wayne Booth, "The Rhetorical Stance," *College Composition and Communication,* 14 (October 1963), p. 141.

89   Theodore M. Bernstein, *Miss Thistlebottom's Hobgoblins: The Careful Writer's Guide to the Taboos, Bugbears and Outmoded Rules of English Usage,* Noonday ed. (New York: Farrar, Straus & Giroux, 1973), p. 189.

90   H. W. Fowler, *A Dictionary of Modern English Usage* (Oxford: Clarendon, 1960), pp. 457–58.

91 Winston Churchill, quoted in Rudolf Flesch, *The Art of Readable Writing,* Collier Books ed. (New York: Collier, 1962), p. 149.

92 George O. Curme, *Syntax* (Boston: D. C. Heath, 1931), p. 459.

93 Bernstein, *Miss Thistlebottom's Hobgoblins,* p. 174.

93 Robert Selph Henry, *The Story of the Confederacy,* rev. ed. (1931; reprint Gloucester, Mass.: Peter Smith, 1970), p. 11.

95 Ernest Hemingway, interviewed by George Plimpton, in *Writers at Work: The "Paris Review" Interviews,* Second Series, ed. George Plimpton (New York: Viking, 1965), p. 222.

96 Donald H. Ross, *The Writing Performance* (Philadelphia: J. B. Lippincott, 1973), p. 24.

101 Rudolf Flesch, *The Art of Plain Talk* (London: Collier-Macmillan, 1962), p. 108.

104 Mark Twain, "Autobiography," *The Portable Mark Twain,* ed. Bernard DeVoto (New York: Viking, 1968), p. 619.

104 Twain, "Pudd'nhead Wilson's Calendar," *Pudd'nhead Wilson,* ch. 5.

105 Leon Edel, "Literature and Biography," *Relations of Literary Study: Essays on Interdisciplinary Contributions,* ed. James Thorpe (New York: MLA, 1967), p. 62.

106 Eric F. Goldman, *The Tragedy of Lyndon Johnson* (New York: Knopf, 1969), p. vii.

111 Charlie Chaplin, interview in *Life* magazine, 10 March 1967.

111 H. L. Mencken, quoted in Nolte, *Mencken,* p. 50.

112 C. S. Lewis, *Letters of C. S. Lewis,* ed. W. H. Lewis (New York: Harcourt, Brace, 1966), p. 127.

112 Melvin Maddocks, review of *Max Jamison* by Wilfrid Sheed, *Life* magazine, 15 March 1970.

112 Gale Hickman, letter to the author.

112 Sammy Davis, Jr., with Jane and Burt Boyar, *Yes I Can: The Story of Sammy Davis, Jr.* (New York: Pocket Books, 1966), p. 130.

112 Mark Twain, *A Treasury of Mark Twain,* ed. Edward Lewis and Robert Myers (Kansas City: Hallmark, 1967), p. 48.

113 J. William Fulbright, *The Arrogance of Power* (New York: Random House, 1966), p. 5.

115 Joseph Wood Krutch, *If You Don't Mind My Saying So* (New York: W. Sloane, 1964), p. 128.

116 Woody Allen, *Getting Even* (New York: Warner Paperback Library, 1972), p. 19.

116 Jo Coudert, *Advice from a Failure* (New York: Stein & Day, 1965), p. 156.

116 Barbara Tuchman, "Can History Use Freud? The Case of Woodrow Wilson," *The Atlantic Monthly* (February 1967), p. 44.

116 Corey Ford, "The One and Only W. C. Fields," *Harper's* magazine, October 1967.

117 Stephen Spender, "The Making of a Poem," *Partisan Review,* Summer 1946.

117 Eliot Fremont-Smith, review of *Language and Silence: Essays on Language, Literature, and the Inhuman* by George Steiner.

117 William Fankboner, letter to the author.

118 H. L. Mencken, *The Vintage Mencken,* ed. Alistair Cooke (New York: Vintage, 1955), p. 233.

118 Ken Macrorie, *Telling Writing* (New York: Hayden, 1970), p. 250.

121 J. V. Fleming, in a lecture given at Princeton University, quoted in the *Princeton Alumni Weekly* (October 30, 1973), p. 10.

121 Twain, *A Treasury of Mark Twain,* p. 59.

121 Orwell, "Politics and the English Language," p. 91.

122 Twain, *A Treasury of Twain,* p. 6.

122 H. L. Mencken, quoted in Nolte, *Mencken,* p. 49.

123 Oscar Wilde, *The Importance of Being Earnest,* Act I.

124 Fulbright, *The Arrogance of Power,* p. 3.

124 Schjelderup-Ebbe, quoted in Anthony Storr, *Human Aggression* (New York: Atheneum, 1968), p. 25.

128 H. L. Mencken, quoted in Nolte, *Mencken,* pp. 62, 102.

129 Jacques Barzun, *Teacher in America,* Anchor Book ed. (Garden City, N.Y.: Doubleday, 1959), p. 47.

131 Ezra Pound, *ABC of Reading* (New York: New Directions, 1951), p. 32.